SILENCED
NO
MORE

SILENCED NO MORE

Surviving My Journey to Hell and Back

SARAH RANSOME

HarperOne
An Imprint of HarperCollinsPublishers

Names and identifying characteristics of some individuals have been changed.

Cover photo background: The photo was taken in October 2019 by a French journalist who accompanied Sarah to the door of Jeffrey Epstein's apartment in Paris months after his death, when she had summoned the courage to confront his enablers. The photo shows her ringing the bell. Although she confronted the staff for their complicity in what they had presumably witnessed there, the staff essentially laughed in her face.

HarperCollins books may be purchased for educational, business, or sales promotional use. For information, please email the Special Markets Department at SPsales@harpercollins.com.

FIRST HARPERCOLLINS PAPERBACK PUBLISHED IN 2022

Designed by Terry McGrath

Library of Congress Cataloging-in-Publication Data is available upon request.

ISBN 978-0-06-321370-8

22 23 24 25 26   LSC   10 9 8 7 6 5 4 3 2 1

Contents

The Story

There is no greater agony than
bearing an untold story inside you.

—MAYA ANGELOU

I never planned to tell The Story. On the day in 2007 when I fled hell, I made a pact with myself: no one would hear the details of what happened to me during the most grievous nine months of my life. Not my parents. Not my brother. Not even my close friends. The den of depravity I had endured was too horrendous, too grisly ever to breathe aloud. Sharing The Story would resurrect it, I felt, revive a nightmare I intended to keep buried. And there it lay, entombed for a long while, bathed in darkness, quiet, shame. Until, after nearly a decade underground, it unexpectedly stirred.

The Story, my horror, isn't one you know. What you've witnessed is the landscape, the sweeping panorama of press reports. In July 2019, billionaire financier Jeffrey Epstein was charged with operating one of history's most vast and seamy sexual assault networks. A month later, he was dead, ostensibly because he'd hanged himself in his prison cell. The next summer, Jeffrey's chief accomplice, British socialite Ghislaine Maxwell, daughter of the late disgraced media tycoon Robert Maxwell, was taken into custody by the FBI at the New Hampshire house where she'd wrapped her cell phone in tinfoil, seemingly to evade detection. Together, she and Jeffrey are accused of recruiting, grooming, and irrevocably damaging at least a hundred girls, many of them underage. Those are the facts we've all taken in.

My testimony lurks between those headlines, in the spaces surrounding the summaries. It's the close-up lens on a torture no Epstein and Maxwell survivor has ever published. It's the narrative record of what happened in Jeffrey's sprawling Fifth Avenue mansion. Onboard his Lolita Express, the 727 he used to transport countless girls into Hades. On his Pedophile Island, the Caribbean hideaway I once risked my life trying to escape. It's the truth about what I experienced at the vile hands of Ghislaine, how she starved and berated and swindled me while demanding I be raped daily—claims, like all others made against her, she categorically denies. That is the appalling chronicle you don't know, the heartache now demanding to be aired. I share it not for voyeurism's sake but because remedying injustice begins with confronting it.

The Story, once roused, asked questions most disquieting. How does a twenty-one-year-old college dropout like Jeffrey weasel his way into a job at an elite prep school where his female students, way back in the 1970s, noted his lecherous gaze? How could Jeffrey and Ghislaine operate a rape pyramid scheme for twenty-plus years, all as the powerful leaders they hobnobbed with didn't notice, didn't care, or became involved and thus feared retribution?

How did an unsuspecting young woman like me, the grandchild of a wealthy British baron who rubbed elbows with Ghislaine's father, become ensnared in this web of perversion? And how can Ghislaine, along with three other women involved in my abuse, now claim to have known nothing about the assaults I actually witnessed them orchestrating? Some of these questions still confound me. All, among others, I'll explore.

In a world where a lot of lip service is given to female empowerment—where sisters stand arm in arm in the name of #MeToo and #TimesUp—Jeffrey employed scores of women in carrying out his crimes. Some of those he abused became abusers, putting forward their own families as his casualties. This master puppeteer, crafty as he was, couldn't have sustained this transatlantic operation on his own. In addition to the enablers whose silence he purchased, Jeffrey had the alliance of a tribe of women who, as they profited, knew precisely what was happening to the girls they sent him. I was lured by such a woman into Jeffrey's crosshairs, on a day I now wish I could do over.

You'll read much, in these pages, about the process of grooming—how connivers woo victims by first forging an emotional connection, how they maintain control through threats and carrot dangling. In our yearslong conversation on sexual violation, our culture hasn't yet truly grasped the nuances of that conditioning. We understand it in broad strokes: an antagonist sets a trap, a hapless deer wanders in. But many don't absorb the particulars. They don't recognize how a perpetrator sniffs out the most vulnerable prey, how a would-be victim actually emanates despair. They don't realize just how frequently assailants sit at our dinner tables—not the Stranger Dangers we spot coming, but the charmers we've grown to trust. Then when a survivor discloses her abuse, some forget the manipulation and look instead at her skirt length. What was she doing in a club? How much cleavage did she bare, how red was her lipstick, how high were her stilettos? *She brought it on herself,* the thought often goes. *She flirted, drank too much, asked for it.*

A certain kind of woman is most likely to be believed—the chaste, the young and doe-eyed, the white, and the heterosexual. I aim to widen the circle of whom we deem credible. I've made regretful choices in the name of survival and acted, at times, in breathless desperation. I am not perfect, and that is the point. I want to encourage a culture in which survivors, even if they haven't led spotless lives, even if they're not proud of all their behavior, still feel the right to stand in their truth. Because while we're in rapidly changing times, when more and more sufferers are daring to speak up, rape remains one of the most underreported violent crimes across the globe. If only the fully virtuous deserve a hearing, then no one born human should ever have a day in court.

The Story that follows is all my own: at turns raw and revolting, lilting and unmeasured. It's an account not just of trafficking and sexual subjugation but of generational patterns, of spirits passed down from parent to child, of songs and prayers whispered in the dark. It is the memory of a girl, lost and utterly broken, who leaned on her faith and somehow found her voice. It's the secret I've kept hidden in my heart's back room until courage, one morning, finally shook it awake.

Part I

LOST

I no longer believe that people are born
without virtue. It gets beaten out. Misfortune threshes
our souls as a flail threshes wheat, and the lightest
parts of ourselves are scattered to the wind.

—DANIELLE TELLER in *All the Ever Afters:
The Untold Story of Cinderella's Stepmother*

1

Heirs and Errs

The Story does not start with my beginning. Its genesis is decades in the making, stretching back to before my mom was banished from her father's palatial Essex estate and sent to South Africa. It commences earlier than when Mum inherited her mom's anguish, before whiskey loosened her tongue and dimmed her light. It also started prior to the era when my grandpa and his father mingled with British royalty. Still, I will begin there. Because you'll never understand how I stumbled into Jeffrey and Ghislaine's hell until you glimpse the one that paved my way to it.

Power flows paternally in my family. My maternal grandfather was the late Honorable Lord James Gordon Macpherson, 2nd Baron of Drumochter, a member of the UK Parliament, and a multimillionaire. He was the only son and thus heir to the fortune of his father, Thomas Macpherson, 1st Baron of Drumochter—a Scottish businessman, Labour Party politician, and chairman of Macpherson Train and Co. Limited. My great-grandfather amassed his wealth by importing and exporting food and produce. He reared his three children—my grandpa and his two sisters—in a *Downton Abbey*-type estate in Brentwood, Essex, amid the high-society sensibilities he passed on to his offspring.

My grandfather's boyhood was bookended by global battles. He was born in 1924, six short years after the close of the Great War, which shifted the world's political tectonic plates and redrew its map. The cultural, political, and social tremors were felt throughout my grandpa's early years as his homeland mourned its losses. Though the British Empire had extended its territory during the clash, it also drained its resources and weakened its stance as a superpower. The First World War, the conflict meant to end all others, failed spectacularly in that respect. Just as my grandpa came of age, he and his countrymen were called on to fight in the Second World War. He served as a tail gunner, spraying the enemy with machine-gun fire. It was in the military that Grandpa met the demure and stunning Ruth Coulter—also known as my grandmother.

Ruth, daughter of a Scottish reverend, was a Wren (Women's Royal Naval Service). I'm not sure what my grandparents saw in each other—other than Ruth's enviable facial bone structure and Gordon's strong pedigree—but they fell hard and fast. My grandmother knew of my grandpa's reputation as an unapologetic womanizer. She also knew that she loved him, as is obvious when I stare at old, faded photos of them, their smiles wide as heaven, their gazes fixed on each other as if nothing else existed. They married in spring 1947. Soon after, they welcomed their son, the Honorable Thomas Ian. My auntie, the Honorable Wendy Shona Coulter, came along in 1950. Three years later, destiny graced them yet again with my mother, the Honorable Shirley Elizabeth. My mother is the baby.

Opulence governed Mum's girlhood. She was outfitted like royalty, in hand-smocked dresses and ankle socks. Her mom donned elegant furs and diamond brooches, hosted extravagant dinner parties among the see-and-be-seen set, spent liberally on fine furniture and art. Members of the royal court, alongside power brokers and politicians, were often seated beneath the crystal chandeliers of Ruth's table. Soirees went into the wee hours, with the men chortling over Scotch and headlines, as the women traded gossip betwixt notes wafting from the phonograph. My grandpa, dignified and with a commanding presence, drove luxury cars, eliciting gapes from those who respected him, feared him, or both. All in the community knew him. He and Ghislaine's dad, press baron Robert Maxwell, served in Parliament. They were contemporaries, if not friends, and they were definitely acquainted in their shared elite circle. They might have shuddered to realize that, decades later across the pond, their heirs' lives would intersect and combust.

I've often wondered whether my grandfather loved being feared. Judging by the sternness of his brow, the stiffness in his jaw, he seemed to. He was a man of so few words that it's difficult to know what he felt. I pondered, too, how his intense war service had pressed its boot down on Grandpa's neck, put a chokehold on his spirit. You can't be a tail gunner and not have PTSD. He seldom spoke about his time in the military, except for once, when he said to my mom, "If you thought the Germans were bad, the Japanese were even worse." Was he tortured? None of us is certain. But his rare statement on the topic spoke volumes about what he had probably endured. It also told me that my grandfather's tough demeanor likely belied tremendous distress.

Mum, like her dad, grew up with everything, except for the one thing she craved most—a connection. Mum felt lost and neglected, as adrift as I would one day feel. She and her siblings were reared by nannies and governesses, a typical arrangement among aristocrats. My mom, who never heard "I love you" from either of her parents, yearned for them to pull her close. She vied constantly for their attention, to no avail. Through the lens of today's norms, my grandparents appear callous, even cruel. But they were creatures of their times, products of their culture. In their upbringings, stoicism upstaged sentiment, solemnity eclipsed expression. What mattered was etiquette. Image. A stellar education at a prestigious boarding school. Speaking the Queen's English with a posh accent. Designer handbags, flawless curtsies, and fancy holidays. The smidgen of affection my grandparents bestowed fell on Tommy, Mum's brother—the eldest, the heir, the one carrying on the Macpherson peerage, and hence their golden child. In the sibling hierarchy, Mum was all but invisible. She might've been born with a silver spoon in her mouth, but its stem, like her heart, was irreparably fractured and tarnished.

My grandmother's poisonous tongue did not help. "What an ugly girl you are," she'd sneer at my mom. "Your sister is the pretty one." It aches to write that sentence, though not half so much as it aggrieved my mother to live it. Mum, brunette and reticent, languished in the shadow of Wendy, a blonde extrovert. In my grandmother's view, her elder daughter was the fairer of the two.

To my eye, they were both gorgeous, though Mum's was the classic beauty, more Audrey Hepburn than Marilyn Monroe. My grandmother's comments stoked acrimony between the sisters, a fact all the more unfortunate since Mum looked to Wendy as a maternal figure. In the absence of Ruth's tenderness, Wendy was the closest thing she had to warmth. My aunt, while herself enduring the insults meted out in that home, did her best to look after her baby sister.

Some wounds heal. Others fester indefinitely. The injuries that continue to pulsate for my mother align with those that destroyed her family. The first, the most agonizing, came the year Tommy was sixteen. He was pedaling his bicycle up a hill when, for an adolescent thrill, he grabbed hold of a truck's rear bumper. The joyride turned catastrophic. Tommy's body hurtled through the air, and he landed, helmetless, on his head. He lay bleeding on the roadside for hours before a passerby spotted him and rushed him to the hospital. But help had come too late. Tommy was brain damaged and confined to a wheelchair, so mentally handicapped he could not intelligibly speak. My grandfather put him in a care facility. Tommy stayed there until his death, years later, from pneumonia. He was thirty when he died.

The blow crippled every person in the family, in ways unique and incalculable. My grandpa coped by disconnecting. Not only was he devastated at essentially losing his only son, his successor, his patriarchal jewel. But he was also mortified by Tommy's disabilities in a society valuing appearance above all else. Of course, Grandpa had the money to care for my uncle at the estate, but doing so would have reminded him of his twin horrors: the great heartache of his heir slipping away, and the great shame he felt over his son's condition. That's why he hid Tommy in a care home he never visited. That's also why he withdrew further inward emotionally.

Grandpa escaped as well by traveling, often on hunting trips abroad. He had always jetted from one country to the next, just as he'd often indulged his adulterous appetites both at home and while on the road. But after Tommy's crash, my grandfather's journeys spanned longer periods and his flagrant infidelities became more frequent. I grew up hearing the scuttlebutt that my grandpa allegedly had an affair with Princess Margaret, queen of Mustique Island and sister to the most royal highness in the British Commonwealth. My grandfather's claimed dalliance, says Mum, was one of scores.

My granny completely lost the plot after her son's tragedy. She had already been a heavy smoker and drinker, deadening her marital woes with alcohol and nicotine. Her reliance on both increased markedly once misfortune struck. For years, she scarcely left her bedroom. By 9 a.m., she was usually downing her first shots of vodka or Bloody Marys; by noon, she was sometimes blacked out. To this day, my mom—who has struggled with alcoholism and drinks wine, gin, rye—will not touch vodka. Its connection to her mom's downward spiral is triggering. Mum recalls the day her mother, plastered and slurring, showed up to a high school sporting event in her nightie. Mum had to usher her swaying, inebriated mother back to her car and off to the estate. The memory stings.

The family's next wound resulted from the first. In 1974, ten years after Tommy was maimed, my grandmother, then fifty, succumbed to throat cancer—a condition caused by her smoking and drinking. She died, too, of a broken heart. While her mother had been deteriorating, Mum had absorbed another agony. At eighteen, she had become engaged to a man she later discovered was sleeping with her best friend and bridesmaid. The nuptials were hastily called off, and her fiancé married the other woman. The betrayal flattened mom. Then, after my grandmother's death, my grandpa tossed a similar dagger. As Grandma lay suffering, my grandfather had begun a long-standing affair. This time he carried on with Catherine Bridget MacCarthy—a friend of my mother and my aunt, the daughter of the family doctor, and a woman far younger than he. Cathy's father was my grandpa's golf buddy. Six months after my grandmother died, my grandfather and Cathy wed. They relocated to the Kyllachy House, a sprawling shooting estate in the Scottish Highlands. My grandpa, without flinching, had slammed the door on his first life and strode toward his second. In 1979, after bearing two daughters, Cathy had a son—and my grandfather had his new heir, the Honorable James Anthony Macpherson, 3rd Baron of Drumochter.

As you can imagine, my mom, and auntie were none too pleased with this turn of events. In fact, Mum has never gotten over the family's series of pummels. She hadn't been close to her brother, Tommy, given their five-year age difference and birth order, but she was nonetheless acutely affected by how his accident altered the family terrain. And despite Mum's emotional distance from her mother, her decline was also excruciating. Mum's outrage at the subsequent wound—her father's disloyalty to his wife's memory and his blatant disregard for my mother's and aunt's feelings—got her nearly disowned.

My mother frowned on her father's affair with Cathy, a disapproval she voiced while my grandmother was still alive. "The trouble with you, Daddy, is that you're completely cunt stuck," she had snapped. He didn't punish her with words. Instead, he shipped her off to South Africa when she was nineteen. Loring Rattray, a friend of my grandpa's, owned MalaMala Game Reserve, well northeast of Johannesburg. Loring and his wife, Natalie, became Mum's guardians. That lasted about two years. Mum, shattered by her upbringing, ailing over her mother's worsening condition thousands of miles away, predictably began drinking and acting out. The fed-up couple sent her packing.

Mum became homeless. My grandpa had given her a modest sum before dismissing her to another continent, but that money ran out. Her father, still roiling with fury at her impertinence, refused to give her more—even after my mother, at twenty-one, limped home for her mom's funeral, for the ceremonial severing of the umbilical cord. But my grandfather had moved on to his happily ever after and had no need to bother with a troubled daughter. So my mother, in a precipitous class descent, ended up living on the beach in Durban for a few months.

Calling on her father's survivor spirit, Mum made her way to Jo'burg and earned money by selling encyclopedias door-to-door. She then somehow landed a job at an advertising agency. While there, she met my father, Mark William Ransome, a fellow Brit reared in Jo'burg, a graphic designer who also worked in advertising. After a two-year courtship, he and my mother wed in 1978, when my mom was twenty-five, a year older than Dad. Mum mended fences with her father well enough to receive his blessing on the matrimony. I get dizzy hearing about Mum and Grandpa's on-again, mostly off-again rounds of reconciliation. During one of those fleeting moments when the air was clear, my parents married on my grandfather's estate. They began their lives together back in South Africa, the cradle of humanity.

I know just two things for sure about my father's background. The first is that he is the youngest of four and thus massively spoiled. The second is that, while his parents were of moderate wealth, his early years were nothing like my mom's affluent ones. As far as my grandfather was concerned, the Ransomes were commoners. Mum recalls the day her father made that plain, when she and my dad visited Grandpa's Kyllachy estate. My grandfather and Cathy hosted a banquet for the occasion. At the table, my father sliced the cheese incorrectly, a significant faux pas in royal etiquette. Dad, bless him, had no clue just how greatly he'd violated a cherished social grace. Grandpa absolutely annihilated my father in front of the large group gathered. My dad's face turned bright crimson as he mumbled an apology.

I know even less about my parents' romance than I do about Dad's upbringing. I'm still untangling what drew them to each other. My mother insists they were deeply in love. My father says he asked Mum to marry him to keep her from committing suicide, which she had threatened. Their recollections aren't mutually exclusive, and the latter is believable given Mum's wrenching girlhood. After my parents exchanged vows, they moved into a nice house in the Bryanston suburb of Jo'burg, and later to the neighborhood of Craighall. They financed their life with their jobs in advertising; both then worked at the same agency. Three years into their union, they started a family. First came my brother, James. Then came me.

"The gods visit the sins of the fathers upon the children," the Greek philosopher Euripides once observed. *All children? Just vices, or also virtues? Only patriarchs, or child bearers as well?* We're left to contemplate. What's evident in my tribe is perhaps apparent in yours. In the story of my family, our behaviors over generations reveal distinct tendencies—recurring narrative threads stitched into our history and genetic code, an emotional inheritance as real as any monetary one. Particularly in the Macpherson lineage, the disparate through lines are visible: Detachment and determination. Abandonment and audacity. Betrayal and resilience. Such plotlines form and frame our lives. The chronicles we're birthed into have everything to do with who we are, what we dream of, and which ancestral spirits weigh us down or urge us onward. Into my family's epic tale I was born—my beginning, yes, but by no means the start of The Story.

2

Things Unseen

I am a stallion at heart. My spirit gallops freely and rebelliously amid the hills, with no regard for rocks and ravines, with wind rippling through its black mane. I come by this trait honestly. My mother long ago outgrew the shyness of her girlhood and thinks nothing, despite her genteel rearing, of extending a middle finger at anyone who crosses her. My late grandmother, though seemingly fragile for periods, nevertheless bucked up under war, both the one on behalf of her homeland and the one in her marriage. Recalcitrance, and its sister, bravery, have many faces. The one I showed at birth was nearly overlooked.

I made it here in 1984 but almost did a U-turn. Dusk was falling on the bustling streets of Jo'burg when Mum, rushed to the hospital by my father after her water broke surprisingly early, pushed me out in concert with her screams. I was quite premature, spending a mere six months and ten days in the womb. Tiny in stature yet mighty in resolve, I had not a single hair on my head and also no eyelashes or brows—ironic given the wild bush growing from my pores now, but not shocking given how early I'd arrived. I shrieked bloody hell at first, and then, suddenly, I began to whimper. The doctors huddled and spoke in hushed tones.

Several medical tests later, the obstetrician delivered his frightening prognosis. "Mrs. and Mr. Ransome," he said, "it looks like your daughter will be dead by morning." He obviously knew nothing of a stallion's nature. I was placed in an incubator as my poor parents, brows furrowed and lower lids welling, stared on helplessly through the plastic dome. With defiance coursing through my arteries and my ancestry, I willed myself through the ordeal. Two weeks into my battle to be here, Mum and Dad at last carried me home. On that bright August day, my brother, James, officially had his only-child card revoked. His baby sister, three years his junior but no less stubborn, had arrived—and *survived*. I'm still doing exactly that.

The land I settled into, fittingly for me, is a fierce underdog of a nation, steely-spined and resolute, a republic determined to rise above its traumas and arch its back toward authentic healing. Countries, like families, have backstories. In the one of my birthplace, the region that reared me, beauty and struggle are salient themes. From the grand Blyde River Canyon in the northeast, to the cream-colored coastlines that put the cape in Cape Town, to the savannahs and waterfalls and wetlands throughout the Rainbow Nation, to the millions of delightful souls scattered across the plains, South Africa inspires awe in even the most jaded sojourner. It also rouses blistering memories, of colonizers plundering and pillaging the land of its rich resources and enslaving its proud people; of a society cordoned off by class and color, and united, for decades, by precious little; of the residual impact of apartheid—Afrikaans for "apartness"—and its wrongs that extend, in various forms, to this moment.

When I turned up in the mideighties, that dehumanizing caste system was still intact. Nelson Mandela, justice's ardent champion, was two decades into his twenty-seven-year prison term at Robben Island, where he lay on a cement floor in a fifty-six-square-foot cell and clandestinely penned his autobiography, *Long Walk to Freedom*. Amid roars of celebration reverberating from the country's impoverished townships, up to its highest point in Lesotho, Mr. Mandela was released on February 11, 1990, the year I turned six. His emergence heralded a much-anticipated ending, as well as a continuing attempt to fully actualize his memoir's title. "As I walked out the door toward the gate that would lead to my freedom," he said, "I knew if I didn't leave my bitterness and hatred behind, I'd still be in prison." While gripping that notion, he stepped out of his past story line and created another.

I had no real understanding of apartheid as a young girl, but I realize now how it touched my world, how its norms conditioned me years before I could articulate that influence. Miriam, my kind Zulu nanny, started working with my family before I was born. The society around me designated her a member of the "Black race," a socially constructed label meant to expel her from the *human* race. Her white neighbors looked down their pointed noses at her African one, regarded her not just as lower in the caste but intellectually and eugenically unfit—a brute deserving of mistreatment, the thinking the Third Reich used to justify sending Jews to the gas chambers. Because of her place in that hierarchy,

Miriam was segregated into a dilapidated township and required to show a passbook to enter our area. Though I now recognize and mourn how Miriam and her entire community were silenced and dismissed on the basis of skin tone, I saw my dear nanny simply through the lens of love.

Miriam was my surrogate mum, full stop. She cradled me, bathed me, fed me, burped me, and held me in her bosom while my parents worked. During the week, she lived in an apartment on our property. On the weekends, she left to be with her family. I believe that she had a husband and children, though I never met them or knew their names. The fact that she shared hardly anything about her personal life, about the miseries and moments that might have brought her to my folks' doorstep, is in itself a statement of how little regard our world held for her, how clearly she understood that her story mattered not in the society beyond her all-Black township. History records the accounts of those who hog the pen, while the marginalized become faint and tiny footnotes, if even recognized. All I can say is that the Miriam I glimpsed, in the untold story intersecting with mine, is a woman who cared for me as if she had birthed me from her own womb. In fact, she would, at heartbreaking moments during my childhood, come to feel like my only mum. In my book, she is a heroine. In these pages, she'll have an encore.

My earliest memory is of my family cracking into two jagged pieces. Before then, I recall only snatches of scenes, the kinds of fuzzy images one sees on an old telly that is badly in need of rabbit ears. But my parents' divorce—that memory comes through with vivid, static-free clarity. I was three and a half. Mum called

James and me into her and my father's bedroom. My parents both sat on their king bed, stone-faced and frigid, with no trace of the emotion that surely led to their jarring news. "We're getting a divorce," Mum said flatly. I began wailing while my brother, distraught to the point of paralysis, stared ahead. Mum embraced me as Dad lowered his eyes. I would later learn that he'd had an affair, slathering salt on Mum's heartache, retracing my grandfather's transgressions. The past is prone to repeating itself, even once we insist that it fade to silence. And seldom, upon reprisal, does it stammer or whisper. In this instance, it bellowed.

After months of rancorous proceedings, my parents' divorce became final on February 17, 1989. Exactly seven days later, Dad married Linda, the woman he'd begun seeing while married to my mum. Linda, stylishly dressed, with green eyes and a short black bob, worked for years as the advertising director of an interior design magazine. Stunningly to me then, yet unsurprisingly in light of what I now know about ancestral templates, the Universe set up the very same dynamic for me that it once had for my mom. Her dad wounded her. So did her husband. My father, inadvertently yet still immensely, injured me in a reminiscent way.

I am a daddy's girl. That's not because I have ever successfully held my father's gaze for any remarkable length of time, but mostly because I hungered for his attention, just as my mum once did for her parents'. As a toddler, I loved crawling into Dad's lap, peering up at his grin, feeling his chest rise and fall when he breathed. One of my favorite old photos is one in which my father holds me in the crook of his elbow as he kisses me gently on the head. It is evidence, amid a paucity of it in my memory, that, yes, Daddy loves me. Yes, Daddy adores his eldest girl. Yes, Daddy *sees* me. That is what I wanted more than anything . . . for him to truly behold me as one would a sight of glorious imperfection. I am sure, in his way and in his view, he has always cherished me. But there stretches a wide canyon between how my father did and did not express his love, and the cheek-to-cheek warmth I needed in order to be assured of his care. That makes neither of our perceptions erroneous. It proves both of us profoundly human.

My father didn't just split with my mother. He also seemingly moved on from James and me as he focused on his new life with my stepmother. They eventually had two children, Robert and Natalie, my half siblings. It's not that Dad didn't visit us in the years right after the divorce. I also have memories, scattered yet fond, of fly-fishing with my father on the river. He loved taking James and me along. He was physically present, especially early on, and he offered us the odd hug. Yet I sensed his gaze elsewhere, as if I no longer stood at the center of his world but had been sidelined to its cold, remote fringes, a township of an emotional sort. Neglect isn't usually announced. It's felt.

Mum remarried as well. After she and my dad went their separate ways, my mother left the advertising agency and launched her own marketing firm, the eponymous Liz Shaw and Associates. While still at the agency and before she hung out her shingle, she had met Matthew, a web developer. Mum and Matthew wed in 1990, when I was six. For financial reasons, my mom had to sell our charming home in Craighall. We relocated to Blairgowrie, a leafy suburb named after a town in Scotland. Mum says she immediately regretted her Round Two of vows. Whatever the issues between her and Matthew, I am certain of this: the union was a disaster. They rowed constantly, with one of their arguments becoming so intense that Matthew—or was it Mum?—fell against, and then out of, a window and had to be hospitalized.

Matthew didn't seem to like my brother. My stepfather, who shot icy stares at James, perhaps was envious of his special place in Mum's heart. My brother was a mama's boy. I, however, got along well with Matthew and was actually fond of him. In hindsight, I recognize that I yearned for a man's strong arms of love and protection, as well as for the Norman Rockwellesque existence that eluded me. Matthew filled that longing, fit into my *Father Knows Best* notion of familial bliss in place of the brokenness I'd experienced. That's why I latched onto him, and every man my mother would eventually bring into our lives. Mum and Matthew's contentious marriage lasted only six years. They divorced in 1996, when I was eleven. Just as I had adapted to my new once-upon-a-time, the final credits were already rolling.

My grandfather, the ghost of abandonments past, felt more like a mythical figure than the flesh of my flesh. Numerous were the stories of his regal Scotland estate and volatile temper; scarce were his visits to Jo'burg. In my early childhood, in the years before a difficult adolescence carried me to my grandfather's foyer, I probably saw him five times, if that. There was no Zoom in that era, no Prince Harry sharing a FaceTime screen with his grandmother, Her Majesty the Queen, from a world away. During the few occasions when Grandpa did come to town, on business or for a hunting holiday, our connection, if it can be called that, was peculiar. I was taught to regard him as royalty—"Yes sir, no sir, thank you very much, sir." That strict protocol left no room for intimacy.

The male presence I most desired moved 786 miles south of me when I was nine. My father and Linda relocated from Jo'burg to Cape Town in 1993. Dad's stated reason for leaving: when the family's nanny took my half brother out for a walk in his pram, a group of men approached her and offered money for Robert because their witch doctor wanted to make medicine of him for use in a ritual. Apparently, the nanny had been followed. They hastily packed up and left for Cape Town. Dad also left James and me.

I regarded that account with a highly raised eyebrow. I still do. Because while I may never know the truth, I felt my dad and Linda wanted, all along, to move to Cape Town, which is where her parents lived. Once she and my father settled into their next chapter, I went from seeing my dad every second weekend to just twice a year, during school holidays. James and I were crushed. Our father departed so abruptly that there was no time for hugs and goodbyes.

We were too young to fly on our own. So my brother and I made our visits via Greyhound bus, just the two of us. I could never sleep during the bumpy, fifteen-hour journey. Instead, I'd peer out my window at the passing Karoo Desert, at the majestic Drakensberg Mountains glistening in the soft light of dawn. Nature then, as it still does, bathed me in comfort. When I am surrounded by trees lifting their arms toward heaven, by rocks and hilltops crying out to their Maker, by ocean currents clapping to declare their praises, I'm convinced there's something bigger than me—an omnipotence unseen yet tangible, a spiritual presence flowing above me, beneath me, inside me. Over and over in the miles ahead, as my motor-coach ride tossed me to and fro, I would ground myself with that inner knowing, that one immutable certainty.

I've never doubted Mum's love. Her care for James and me began years before she even conceived us. She understood all too well a child's pain in craning his or her neck to spot signs of endearment. She lived that. She could not be a perfect mother, she understood, but by God, she'd be full-throated in her assertion: she treasured us to the firmaments and back. In fact, she ladled on the love extra thick, just to be sure we were covered in it. "Come here, you two," she'd say, pulling us into her arms after breakfast. "You know Mummy loves you, right? *Yes, Mum. Absolutely. Eternally.*

Provision was her other form of devotion. She invested long hours in her fledgling business, immersed herself in the effort to keep us clothed, fed, educated. Parents are inclined to want for their children more than they themselves had in childhood, and my mother was no exception. Without the benefit of her father's deep pockets, but with the social privileges her upbringing and society at large graced her with, my mother did well for herself. She received little maintenance, or child support as it is called in America, from my dad. He sent money when he could, and

I acknowledge and appreciate the contribution. It was, however, not sufficient. My father is a gifted artist, a graphic designer and business owner who creates wine labels for wineries and other clients. He's a better artist than he is a salesman and has struggled, at times, to remain solvent. His wife has long been the primary breadwinner and has often bailed him out.

My father's inconsistent support meant that our mother spent more time away from James and me than she would've liked—hence, her overcompensation with displays of sentiment. I'm blessed I never lacked for material basics. She worked her arse off to ensure it. Though her father sat on millions overseas, that money didn't flow Mum's way. When she and my father married and returned to Jo'burg, my grandfather's parting gifts were one ring and a pair of diamond earrings that my grandmother had worn—two items Mum still has, unlike the jewelry of her own she'd eventually need to sell. She wasn't down to her last rand. But in the feast-or-famine reality of entrepreneurship, one cannot predict when a lean time will arrive, or how long it will lie back and make itself at home. If heaven has smiled on you by way of a strand of pearls, you'd do well to pawn it in order to pay your mortgage.

Mum may not have been an heiress to her father's riches, but she held fast to an upper-class tradition: hosting fancy dinner parties. She absolutely loved entertaining, though on a far more modest scale than her own mum had been able to. James and I went mad over the appetizers Mum and Miriam prepared: the pâtés, the sweets, the fruits and cheeses. We'd sneak into the kitchen and munch ourselves silly, until Mum, noticing the vanishing crisps, shooed us away. "You're eating everything up before the guests arrive!" she'd half-scold, half-laugh.

Hours before the doorbell rang, my mother made a full-time job of getting dressed . . . we're talking *ages*. "Mum, can I look at all your jewelry?" I'd plead as I watched her apply her makeup from my spot on her bed. Years earlier, she'd done the same in her mom's dressing room. "Sure," she'd say. Even before her permission, I was giddily trying on beaded necklaces, pearls, the diamond earrings my granny had once worn. "Look, Mum," I'd say, strutting by to show her my pretend studded lobes. "Aren't they *gorgeous*?" She'd glance over and smile, holding her hand steady as she put on mascara.

Mum, once dressed, looked ready for a Paris catwalk. Her makeup was immaculate, as were her red nails. To this day, I love having my nails painted red because it reminds me of my mother in those years. She could transform even the most basic staples and accessories into head-turning ensembles. She may not have owned Chanel or Burberry, but courtesy of her masterful eye, the generic appeared glamorous. She knew what looked good on her and made it work. During the period when Mum first met my dad, he went with her briefly back to the UK, where she enrolled in the acclaimed Champneys Beauty College, Tring. She completed her course but decided against that career path. Yet the training showed in her stunning presentation, both of herself and of the gorgeously arranged spreads adorning our dining table. Her great taste extended to my closet. When I was small, Mum dressed me in stylish outfits and helped me select my looks. My love of fashion came not while poring over British *Vogue* but while admiring my mother's elegance. She personified chicness, just as her mother had. I dreamed of one day emulating both.

The parties were as much fun as the preparations. What kid wouldn't enjoy watching a bunch of adults, dressed to the nines, getting sloshed? James and I snickered as Mum and the others danced, sang off-key, made crude jokes. It was hilarious . . . until it wasn't. As the years stumbled forward, Mum proved she was as much her mom's daughter as I am mine. What afflicted my mother was, of course, different from all that bedeviled Grandma, but their attempt to remedy was the same: by anesthetizing the hurt. In the period immediately after Mum's first divorce, as well as during her marriage to Matthew, Mum became a functional alcoholic—the only kind she could afford to be if she hoped to maintain her business. In her male-dominated industry, drinking was central to the culture. She was constantly entertaining clients and attending networking events. So much socializing hastened her toward addiction.

Her periods of dysfunction are almost too agonizing to recall. After nights out on the town, she'd stagger home, hair scattered, blouse disheveled. Miriam, who looked after James and me, once found my mum passed out in our dog kennel, her legs and high heels jutting from the opening, as our Labrador, Winston, whimpered elsewhere in our backyard. At times, she'd trip across the threshold and then crank up the stereo, blasting Dolly Parton's "I Will Always Love You" for hours, the lyrics intermingling with her sobs, the song's title and refrain uttering the affirmation she'd longed to hear. Her other favorite was Queen's "I Want to Break Free." The next day, Mum never remembered her blackouts or the havoc they'd wreaked.

In that environment, I got little sleep, which affected my studies—or lack thereof. James and I attended the same primary school, I.R. Griffith in Blairgowrie. That changed when my brother, my best friend, an academic star, went off to King Edward VII, a semiprivate all-boys boarding school my mother stretched her savings to pay for. My father contributed what he could. James was thirteen when he enrolled; I was ten and heartsick. James lived on campus during the week. He came home every Saturday morning or afternoon (depending on the school's schedule of sporting events) and returned on Sunday evenings. I didn't have the luxury of living away, and even if I'd had the grades for a top school, I'm certain Mum, regretting the emotional chasm that had separated her from her mother, would have insisted that I stay close.

Later, after completing primary school at age thirteen, I attended Parktown Girls High. I wasn't a great student early on, and I had an even harder time as I got older, partly because I'm dyslexic, and partly because my home life was such a wreck. My brother's weekday world was characterized by structure and discipline. Mine was defined by turmoil amid my mother's intensifying addiction. As my grades slid downhill, so did my behavior. I was a bit naughty in class, courtesy of my inner stallion, and the old-fashioned teachers punished me with their stares and frequent after-school detentions. My mother's reputation as a drunkard and my bad behavior framed their view of me. In their eyes, and in the glares of most of my peers, I was an outcast. They certainly treated me like one, smirking when I entered a room, or whispering about the rye on Mum's breath when she came to parent-teacher conferences.

I'm grateful that, back during primary school, God sent me two bright spots, my best friends Kelly Scates and Kerry Plots. I found solace in their camaraderie and still hold much affection for them. But in high school, my two rocks enrolled elsewhere as I entered Parktown. Gone were the sleepovers and girlfriend giggles that had grounded me. They gave way to a long, gray, adolescent corridor I navigated mostly alone. My brother, on the weekends, helped me with homework when he could, but he understandably just wanted to have fun with his friends. He was growing up, which meant hanging with his little sister wasn't a social priority. I didn't blame him. I just missed him.

In fact, other than my father, I've never missed anybody more than I did James in those years. Not having him there during the week meant I had to deal with Mum's alcoholism on my own. At one point when I was around eleven, after Mum and Matthew divorced, she was drunk more often than she was sober. In that state, she couldn't provide me with the order I craved. Her intent was never to emotionally abandon me. She'd set out to do exactly the opposite of what her mum had been capable of. But as parenting pendulum swings go, Mum propelled hers with such force that it arrived back to its original position. She did not cast me aside. Her addiction did the deserting. Yet even in the grip of intoxication, she insisted on a regimented schedule that Miriam implemented. Homework was to be done after school and completed before I could turn on the telly. Bath time was promptly at 5:30. Dinner and bedtimes were strictly observed. To wiggle out of my math and reading assignments, I'd hand over my pocket money to James so he could tell Mum I'd done them. I'm sure I still owe him some rand.

During my primary school years, as Mum leaned into her habit, I soothed myself by disappearing into an imaginary world, a kingdom far away from my loneliness. I'd assure Miriam that my homework was finished (it wasn't) and pull out my gummy bear snacks (thus spoiling my supper). I'd then escape into my favorite shows: *The Simpsons*, *Rupert the Bear*, *My Little Pony*. I loved the latter so much that Mum bought me the toy, a miniature horse with a multicolored mane and tail. As I played, and as Mum drank herself numb elsewhere in the house, I'd giggle and sing my made-up ditty in place of the theme song: "My little pony, skinny and bony . . ."

I was also besotted with all things Barbie. I had a pink doll-house from the collection, and neither Miriam nor Mum could pull me away from it! When I should've been in bed, I'd be on the floor in the shadows, re-creating a happy family in the beautiful Dutch-style abode, one modeled after those in our area. Barbie was as impeccably dressed as my mum, with a chic outfit for every occasion. I brushed her flowing, golden hair so zealously that she ended up nearly as bald as I'd been at birth. In my fantasy, every-one wanted to be Barbie's friend. She was seen and admired and celebrated. And in my land of fake-believe, in that realm bearing no resemblance to my true one, my father gave a rip. My mom set aside her whiskey tumbler. My family, like that of Barbie's, re-mained forever intact. The day you grow up is the day you grasp the truth: No prince is coming to save you. No magic horse exists. No paradise awaits you somewhere over the rainbow. Life, the sobering reality show, would sear that into my flesh.

3

Front Crawl

Sleep turns its back on the already restless. There are evenings, long stretches between midnight's groan and daybreak's grin, when I find myself ruminating over press clippings on the Epstein-Maxwell case, haunting memories stealing my shut-eye. One path to insomnia came with a comment I read in the 2019 *Vanity Fair* piece "Unraveling the Mystery of Ghislaine Maxwell," by the journalist Vanessa Grigoriadis. In it, she quotes a source close to the socialite. "When I asked what she thought of the underage girls," this friend reportedly recalled of her conversation with Ghislaine, "she looked at me and said, 'They're nothing, these girls. They are trash.'"

Trash. These girls. Nothing. What vexes me about that statement isn't just its apparent savagery, but the entitlement of its premise. I'm familiar with such snobbery, with the human tendency to sneer. My ancestry runs through that landscape. Classism, like all *isms*, attempts to shoo away the flies, rid the room of perceived annoyances, crush the bloody nuisances if necessary. It

gives the swatter, the powerful, sole control of the wire handle—
the right to quash the vulnerable, the pride in purifying the world
of diseased pests presumed inferior. That's how the Holocaust
happened. That's how Jim Crow lynchings and apartheid were
justified, how Dalits became "untouchable," Korean females were
exploited as "comfort women," and Tutsis were reduced to "cock-
roaches" during the Rwandan genocide. You have to demonize
a "nothing" to rationalize tormenting it. And during its anni-
hilation, the assailant seldom even looks at its victim, its trash.
Because if he or she stared, an awareness might dawn that this
nothing has wings. This nothing carries hopes. This nothing once
swam and prayed and loved and feared, delighted in dollhouses
and dreamed of better. And this supposed nothing, at age eleven,
had her soul sliced in half.

Miriam left early that evening. She fed me supper and tucked
me in, assured me Mum would be home soon. My mother and
Matthew had divorced by this time. The split sent Mum into
an alcoholic stupor, one worse than any previous. Her business also sustained tremors. With these fresh agonies, the Pinot
Grigio flowed more freely; with Mum's nights out with this
suitor or that one, Dolly Parton crooned ever louder. I coped
by clinging to my nanny, the bonus mum who's the reason I'm
right side up, the angel my nation vilified because of her color.
I'd often tiptoe from my room and find Miriam in the lounge,
relaxing on the sofa with her tea. "Will you come sit with me?"
I'd whisper. She'd sense my need and set aside her cuppa, read
me stories until my closing lids carried me to tranquility. But
on this Friday she had to get home to her children. That meant I

was alone, under my blanket yet awake, when I heard the front door crash open.

"Please, Lizzie . . . I mean, let's . . ." a stammering male voice said before it trailed off. "That's . . . it's enough, you!" Mum snapped, and by how she sounded, the warbling of her words, I knew she was shit-faced. Footsteps approached in the hall toward my room, interspersed with pleas from my mother, then snipes back and forth, then shouts. They rowed for a while, I can't recall about what, and I clutched my teddy bear. Quiet fell for a moment before my door creaked open. There stood my mom, cheeks ruby, hair rumpled, naked from head to toe. She ambled toward me, nearly tripping but catching herself, and then she slid into the bed beside me. "Let me hug you, darling," she slurred. She reeked of booze. I recoiled a bit, startled by her clammy flesh so close to mine, my mind scrambling to understand what was going on. Seconds later, the man, also nude, crept into the room. Mom sat up. "Get the fuck out of here!" she yelled. He obeyed. Mom rose from my bed, picked up my teddy, and wound it up. As the tune played, she wandered back to her bedroom and collapsed. I drew in a breath and let it out slowly. *It's over.*

It wasn't. Mum's lover returned, nude as before, but this time erect. I'd never seen a penis, much less one in full salute, and it frightened me into wails. He inched toward me. "Leave me alone," I sobbed, clutching my teddy with all my might, scooting to the far edge of my mattress. "Please, stop!" With my every scream, the man drew nearer, his eyes devoid of feeling. He climbed on top of me, pressed his damp palm over my mouth, and forced himself inside me—powerfully enough to rupture my flesh.

Thrust. Thrust. Thrust. Once he'd satisfied himself, he got up and left, as casually as if he were going out for the paper. I quivered atop the sheets, bleeding and sniveling as my bear's lullaby played over and over, as if to offer a musical salve, as if to soothe me the way Dolly Parton did Mum. Some children lose their innocence one increment at a time, in the steady flow of sand through the cinched waist of a timepiece. I lost mine not grain by grain but with the bashing open of the hourglass, the toppling of shards to the floor.

While Mum was passed out the next morning, I laundered my own blood-streaked linens, gown, and undergarments, bleached them of all memory of the transgression, pretended my crotch did not moan in distress. I told no one, not even Miriam. In the naive calculus of my girlhood, I blamed myself. I should've screamed more loudly so Mum could intervene, should've begged my sweet nanny to stay past her shift, should've somehow staved off a 250-pound behemoth with my 70-pounds-and-trembling frame. The shame clasped closed my jaw, choked back my sorrow. To this moment, Mum does not know any detail of what happened to me on that evening, in the shadows, with my bear humming a lament. As a child, I thought it was the most excruciating experience I'd ever endure, the one secret I'd need to keep. I shudder now at how wrong I was.

Trauma, we know, indelibly alters a child's brain. Academic highfliers may suddenly flail. Some—not all—become cutters, bed wetters, nail biters, thumb suckers, panickers, over- or undereaters, hypervigilant and ultrasensitive. The lingering effects of the trenchant violation may manifest as promiscuity, an irksome term used to cast shade on the "bad girl," the one accused of lifting her skirt, with no acknowledgment that a beast first violently yanked it up. The assault embeds beliefs in a survivor's frontal lobe that she has no right to her boundaries, that she isn't safe, that she's dirty and discardable—lies that play out in her friendships, romances, work. Many, like me, escape into a fictional paradise, dissociating from the horror. Secrecy becomes a habit, shame a constant. Injured minors become adults who, though fully grown in body, often remain shivering babes, unable to set words to their requiems, attempting to dull the throbbing in various self-harming ways. Children don't outgrow their traumas. They just grow taller. Trauma changes us on a cellular level.

Beyond short-circuiting the nervous system, abuse burdens the spirit, hangs an albatross around its neck, mutes its tongue, and obscures its light. I was never the same after my terror, in ways I only now comprehend. I'm not talking just about the hurt thrust on me in 1995. I'm also referring to the cumulative battering over generations, the gashes staining my family tree, the fractured bones never plastered and set. I see my own swollen contusions. I also observe, in noon's unsparing light, blisters passed from parent to child, teeth wired shut and screams squelched, muffled cries in the attic of the unconscious. I see injuries, left untreated, that bred others eerily similar. I glimpse The Story in its wretched fullness, in its cringingly unclothed state.

Water speaks to me. Africa, in the natural world, is its own proverbial kettle of fish, with flora and fauna unique to the continent, with jacaranda trees flaunting violet blossoms, with hadada birds calling "kuur, kuur," with wonders that curl up in your spirit and slumber for infinity. Nothing stirs me like the deep blue, the expanse of shimmering turquoise and sapphire, the crisp sea breeze running its fingers through my hair, the tepid tides of the Indian Ocean holding hands with the cold Atlantic down at Cape Point. I've wandered off from the Motherland for long spells, marveled at beauty all over the world. But Africa's waters whisper to me from afar, urging me ever homeward.

When you grow up in a land cradled by currents, with rivers and marshes dotting the terrain, swimming is part of life. In addition to God's numerous dipping pools, many locals maintain their human-made ones, to cool off in summer's unforgiving scorchers. I was still a toddler when Mum put me into our backyard pool. My brother had been given swimming lessons. I, however, was a complete natural from age three, from the moment she chucked me in the water. I've been paddling around so long I can't recall a time when I wasn't out there among the ripples, giggling and splashing my way to joy. In my early years, and intermittently well beyond, swimming rescued me. Water knew my name, pulled me close, saw me when few others did. It sang my freedom.

I didn't just learn to snorkel, float, and tread. I kicked some serious tail in the pool, broke local records and created long-standing new ones. I might have been a pariah in the classroom, but I was a champion in all things aquatic, a gladiator in the pool. Through the end of primary school (middle school in America), I won just about every race I entered, earned so many medals that I lost count, became the Katie Ledecky of my area in Jo'burg. In the

4A medley—butterfly, backstroke, breaststroke, and freestyle—I smashed race after race. My wins were an objective measure of my skill. As a competitive swimmer, you are either fast enough or you aren't, with approval awarded by speed times, not by the subjective glares of peers who don't like the way you smell. The sport, like others, comes with all the ingredients of a great story—every meet has a dramatic beginning, a mercifully short middle, and a breathless, triumphant ending. There is a victor and a roaring crowd to boot. If only life were so tidy, so intent on declaring its losers and winners, its sinkers and survivors.

Though it pained me that my family could rarely make it to my meets—Mum was working her fingertips off; Dad was too far away; James cheered me on until he entered boarding school—I relished the competition. The water was a world unto itself, a universe away from home's bedlam. The pool was my sanctuary. My gold medals were my validation in a life that seldom gazed at me with admiration. If I couldn't have my father's "attagirl" or my mother's twelve-step commitment, I could at least have my one dazzling limelight and a room brimming with gilded trophies. And while Mum and Dad were largely absent for my victory laps, the glints in their eyes told me they were proud.

Underwater swimming is one of life's sublime pleasures. As a youngster, I'd cup on my goggles, plunge down to the pool's cracked floor, practice holding my breath for two *l-o-o-o-ng* minutes, cherish the quiet nothingness, the otherworldly sense of serenity . . . and then—*splash!*—I'd burst up through the surface with my heart thundering away, a nerdy grin spread across my face. My other fondness was for freestyle, also known as the front crawl—the classic swimmer's posture. Its alias may seem a misnomer (Australian swimming phenomenon Dick Cavill once described the stroke as like crawling through water, hence the term), but the move actually propels you forward like none other. There you are, belly southward, legs kicking and arms windmilling, body undulating through the stillness, cold on your back and adrenaline in your veins as you glide forward. *Sailing. Breathing. Crawling. Surviving.*

Good thing I had swimming as an anchor. Starting in 1996, the year I was twelve, the earth beneath me quaked once, then twice, and then a third time. The first was a magnitude 7.0. Miriam, who had grown exhausted with my mother's drunken rampages and their resulting trail of destruction, left our family. One Sunday morning after Mum hosted a dinner party, my nanny came in to find soiled plates and flatware strewn all over the house, alongside cigarette butts and spilled booze that stained the tablecloths and rug. She decided she'd had enough, yet she didn't have the heart to tell me. Instead, she insisted we take a photo together, the one in the center of these pages. On the back of the picture, she scrawled eight words I still mouth quietly to myself in moments of distress: "I love you and will always love you." Two weeks later, she hugged me tight and departed.

Her exit changed everything for me. Through my young eyes, I saw her leaving as abandonment, even called it that for a long time afterward. That was my ancestral wound speaking. With my vision improved by years of self-reflection, I now recognize that Miriam did what I and other trauma survivors often find it difficult to do: protect and prioritize ourselves. Miriam did not desert me. She, for once, chose herself. She moved on to another job, I'm sure, with conditions she could abide. Not everyone who walks out is throwing you away. She was not my actual parent, but a gracious stand-in. She didn't owe me her love. And yet she offered it generously for more than a decade.

The year Miriam left, Mum met Jack, a Brit, and another of my stepdads—though he and Mum did not marry. Jack, a land-scape architect and a man prone to outbursts, moved in with us in the summer of 1996. For the same reasons I had latched onto Matthew, I clung to Jack. He and Mum eventually bought a house that was a four-minute walk from my high school. I'm not sure what my mother first saw in Jack because, whatever it was, she saw gradually less of it given his hours. Jack, a workaholic, labored around the clock, spending weekends and even some holidays in his office, while Mum, probably pining based on her level of liquor consumption, managed alone. She once showed up at his workplace, along with our Labrador—reminiscent of the day my slurring, nightie-wearing grandma turned up at Mum's school.

Jack was humiliated. He was let go soon after, partly because of the strain Mum's cameo put on his relationship with his boss, and also because of his vitriolic temper—one rivaling my grand-father's, and one right at home amid Mum's fireworks. There's no coincidence in such pairings. Fury draws fury, and their explosive relationship lasted three years. Around then, one of Mum's busi-ness partners started his own firm behind her back and siphoned off half her clientele. Jack had known of this plan, says Mum, but hadn't told her because of their deteriorating romance. She got lawyers involved, drained her savings, and bought Jack out of his share of the house. Cue the whiskey.

That whole drama didn't constitute my quake. Miriam's transition marked the start of my internal loss of balance. At thirteen, I began drinking and chain-smoking to deaden my heartache, just as a certain two women in my family tree had. At fourteen, I started waiting tables because my mother—with pulverized savings and a father unwilling to hand her a life jacket—needed me to earn some money. I claimed to be sixteen in order to land the job. The same year I donned my apron, the ground beneath me shook twice more. As I walked home from school, a man pulled up in a car beside me and masturbated himself to ejaculation. I ran home and told my mom and Jack (they were still together at this point). They jumped in the car and chased after him but couldn't catch him. The image of that man jerking off as I fled in terror transported me back to the fear, the sheer helplessness I felt on the night I was attacked in my own bed. I was marked for misfortune, I decided. Years would pass before I unpacked that notion.

A third seismic shift came around that time. The wounded child had grown into the rogue teen, the stallion intent on her own path, a girl with curves and budding cleavage and an illegal waitressing job. I rolled my eyes when my mum, teachers, and others labeled me rebellious. I know now I was pleading, with every puff of my cigarette and swig of my beer, for anyone to see me. Intercede. Care. One evening, I lied to my mother about where I was going and headed to a nightclub with a friend. We both got wasted and my pal left without me. A seventeen-year-old boy offered to drop me off at home, and when I climbed into the back seat, he raped me as his classmate cheered him on. Two days later, I broke down and told Mum, who rang my father. My dad didn't believe my story, he said flatly, though I suspect he just wanted nothing to do with me or the incident. His discrediting, the frigidity in his tone, pierced me in ways that still make me tremble. Weeks later, perhaps as some half-hearted acknowledgment of my story, he sent me sunflowers. They wilted along with my insides.

This second rape was, in many ways, more damaging than the initial. The first had disfigured me privately. But the one I mustered the courage to voice was dismissed by my dad and later pushed underground by the community. When it didn't seem to matter that I'd had my knickers and my dignity ripped away, I decided I must not matter either. That is why the three most powerful words a survivor can hear are "I believe you."

Mum reported the crime, and the police opened an investigation. But the boy's family, one of the most well known and wealthy in Johannesburg, paid the department to make the case disappear. Mum was devastated, and I absorbed the lesson: when you speak up, you will be silenced. Your voice, your account, your wails . . . none of it makes a damn bit of difference, particularly if it'll ding the armor, the image, of society's upper crust. I first learned that lesson in my homeland, a nation with one of the highest sexual violence rates in the world, with 40 percent of women experiencing assault at some point in their lives. I also learned that from my father, the man whose protective wing I sought.

My grades plummeted further, and I had to give up swimming because I couldn't fit it around my work. I confided in the rape counselor the police had referred me to, poured out my anguish. That woman shared my secret with her daughter, my high school classmate, who whispered it to others. I was bullied and blamed, branded with a scarlet *L* for loose. That narrative was reinforced when, at work, both my boss and the bar's owner—ages thirty-seven and fifty-nine, respectively—refused to pay me unless I slept with them. I closed my eyes and did, all the while self-flagellating. A Thai family that ran the restaurant next door realized I was lost and offered to send me to Thailand for their extended family to look after me. It was a thinly veiled attempt at sex trafficking.

In desperation one evening just before Christmas, I tried to take my life, swallowed all of Mum's sleeping pills, sobbed and gagged as the capsules became lodged in my throat. I didn't want to die. I wanted to flee my cesspool of a life for a livable existence, find a kingdom of quiet like the one underwater. More than anything, I longed for anyone—and my father in particular—to even slap me upside the head, as evidence I merited, at a minimum, harsh attention. I knew then, as I did when I was younger, that Mum adored me. But her love, steeped in the pain of her own brokenness, fell short. Ours is an odd dynamic, in which I've been more Mum's caretaker than her daughter, the role she played in her mom's life after her brother's accident. I begged my dad to let me come live with him in Cape Town. He and my stepmother declined profusely. Do I grasp, from adulthood's vantage point, why embracing a wayward daughter would be a headache? Yes. Do I wish my dad had been willing to endure that migraine? With all my heart. I'm sure he had a big picture I couldn't understand, had his reasons for distancing himself. When he stepped into his new life, perhaps his previous one became an afterthought. Whatever his rationale, I was leveled. At fourteen, I felt dumped in the trash and forced into survival mode.

I lay bare The Story with two intentions. The first is to cut off the secret's circulation by unearthing it. Daylight is shame's kryptonite. The second aim led me to write this book: connecting all the dots. Airing a crushing blow is cathartic and necessary to healing. I've done that. I do that. Yet my most potent elixir has come with recognizing the history I was born into—the emotional and spiritual legacies I inherited, the rings in my family's oak that reveal pernicious patterns—with the purpose of growing more healthy ones. Years can be spent stewing in resentment and never moving forward. I've lived that misery. The temptation, always, is to slide back into suffering, even to unknowingly create mayhem because that's what is familiar. Chaos reared me. It knows my address, hums my tune, plays a D-minor dirge while making harmony sound off-key, simply because it's foreign to my ear. Decades-long churning is an exercise in remaining mired. Dot connection, for me, has been about progressing beyond the inciting injury, about front-crawling my way to some semblance of healing.

Trauma has an odor. After my first rape, I rehearsed the trio of lies that ran on a loop through my head: *You are damaged goods. You are to blame. You are worthless.* Those beliefs showed up in the way I behaved, dressed, entered a room, everything. Without realizing it, I was broadcasting my brokenness. It didn't need to be stated. It could be nosed out and targeted. The scent of blood attracts predators. They can smell vulnerability, feel the energy of desolation. They can easily spot the "nothings," as Ghislaine apparently did for years.

Maria Farmer can attest. The artist, who once worked as Jeffrey's receptionist—and who says she was sexually assaulted by both him and Ghislaine in 1996—had a front seat to the socialite's modus operandi. She revealed it during her 2019 *CBS Sunday Morning* interview with cohost Anthony Mason. "Did you see young women coming into the house?" Anthony asked. "Yes, I saw many, many, many, many, many," Maria said. "All day long. I saw Ghislaine going to get the women. She went to places like Central Park. I was with her a couple of times in the car. . . . She would say, 'Stop the car.' And she would dash out and get a child." Anthony dug deeper. "What did she say she was doing when she did this?" he said. "Getting Victoria's Secret models," Maria said.

The scary movie doesn't end there. When Maria tried to flee after her own attack, Ghislaine allegedly uttered what the painter interpreted as a threat. "She says, 'You're going out to jog on the West Side Highway every day, and I know this. You need to be very careful because there's so many ways to die there. So you have to be really careful. Look over your shoulder.'" Maria's younger sister, Annie Farmer, also says she was exploited at age sixteen. The two filed complaints with the FBI a full decade before an investigation was opened. In the 2019 *Guardian* piece titled "'She Was So Dangerous': Where in the World Is the Notorious Ghislaine Maxwell?" Maria notes how the socialite cast her spell. "Ghislaine was key in making me feel safe," she said. "I trusted her because she is a woman. She would make us trust her, and she would make us really care about her. My sister even said that she would feel so special if Ghislaine paid attention to her because she had that way about her, you know, the popular girl in school, she was one of those. She knew everybody." Maria says she was assailed at the Ohio estate of Lex Wexner, Jeffrey's billionaire client. She recalls the day Ghislaine rode up on a horse there. "She's got the whole equestrian attire," she says. "She's so elegant"—a wolf disguised in boots and breeches.

Ghislaine homed in on precisely the type of girl she knew she could trap. Trauma is, at times, scantily clad. It draws the stares of assailants who know they are more likely to capture an injured prey than a healthy one. Ghislaine hails from a world like my grandfather's, a country-club circle brimming with beautiful women who have modeling potential, not that Ghislaine's true goal was ever to discover the next Gisele Bündchen. And yet her scavenging reportedly led her to Central Park, in search of girls and young women who might salivate at her proposition. She aimed her arrow with calculation. A child who has been taught her worth, who has a strong voice, is not so easily picked off, particularly if she comes from money. That sort of girl would probably recoil if a stranger, even a well-groomed one, approached her in a park. She'd likely report it to her parents. Ghislaine hunted victims who'd already internalized their "nothingness." Such a child believes at her core that she *should* be abused. Such a child is easy to discern.

It took the accounts of dozens of such girls—the Palm Beach

teens who told police they were groomed and sexually violated by Jeffrey Epstein, with many asserting they were lured by Ghislaine and overseen by Jeffrey's longtime assistant, Sarah Kellen—to first put the billionaire in the FBI's hot seat in 2005. That chair turned out to be a rather comfortable recliner. The financier was given a sweetheart deal in exchange for pleading guilty to state charges of the solicitation and procuring of prostitutes, a term sullying the girls' reputations more than Jeffrey's. That aligns with the playbook used by some in the ruling class: subtly, and then overtly, discredit any victim who dares to speak truth to power. *They are hookers*, often goes the thinking after an accuser has been besmirched. *They deserved what they got.* Jeffrey's extraordinarily lenient eighteen-month sentence in the county jail gave him the right to leave his cell six days a week, twelve hours at a time, to continue working—and raping with impunity.

That wrist slap was as brief as it was gentle. The most dangerous pedophile in modern history served only thirteen months before his release in July 2009, when, on the grounds of good behavior, he was put on a loosely monitored house arrest during which he flew in victims to provide him with sexual services. He also jetted off to his private Caribbean island, trading his feigned detention for a beach holiday. Had the Department of Justice risen to its mission—and had Alexander Acosta, then US attorney general for the Southern District of Florida, insisted on a federal prosecution, rather than punting the case to the state attorney—I and others never would have been trafficked and brutalized.

I first crossed paths with Jeffrey in 2006, when he was already on the FBI's radar, during a period when Ghislaine has claimed she was phasing out of her work with Jeffrey. My photos of her in this book, snapped in December 2006 on the eve of the new year, spin a dramatically different tale. Not only was she still actively partnering with the sociopath then and into 2007; she was frolicking on his island patio with Jean-Luc Brunel, the then-prominent modeling agent who now rots in a French prison, accused of sexual assault, rape, and human trafficking of women and underage girls. I know she was there because I was on Orgy Island that long week. I also know this: Ghislaine loomed at the epicenter of Jeffrey's sordid world, at the cross section of corruption, money, power, and barbaric cruelty.

Much as her family and legal team have tried to soften her image, I see Ghislaine as Jeffrey's female equivalent. That is not because she committed his every heinous act but because she aided and abetted in the most contemptible one. For nearly a decade, she betrayed females, among them girls as young as fourteen. She used her Mary Poppins–like vivaciousness, her Queen's English, and her silver-spooned upbringing to entice these guileless lambs into a lion's den where she knew they would be devoured. Her brother, Ian Maxwell, has attempted to put distance between Ghislaine and the late serial sex offender. "They're taking it out on my sister," Ian told ABC News during a March 2021 interview with James Longman. He described her conditions as "monstrous" in the federal detention center where she awaited trial. "Damn it, that's wrong. She is not Epstein. Epstein was guilty. He did time. And he was gonna do a hell of a lot more time. But she is not him. And I don't know how many times I have to say it. She deserves to be treated as Ghislaine, presumed innocent, get on with the defense, tell us what you've gotta tell us, put it up, and then let the jury decide."

Ian and I agree on one point: his sister, like all of us, should be granted a fair hearing, with full innocence presumed until proved otherwise. Many of the abused won't have that privilege because they're too frightened to ever raise their voices. Whether there is a verdict, and however the case concludes, Ghislaine is, in fact, guilty of devastating me and scores of others. Don't let her re-fined English accent, her charm and pedigree, her social graces and contrived grin deceive you as they have so many. The Loch Ness Monster lurks beneath. And when this raven-haired brute helicoptered into my world, she destroyed what was left of my soul. I alone can testify to that.

Speaking of demolitions, Acosta truly mucked things up for us survivors. With Jeffrey's 2008 plea bargain, the US attorney green-lighted a nonprosecution agreement (NPA) that shielded Jeffrey's known and unknown co-conspirators for all crimes committed between 2001 and 2007 in Florida's Southern District. The hench-women named in the initially sealed NPA: Sarah Kellen, Jeffrey and Ghislaine's right-hand lieutenant; Adriana Ross, the former Polish model who allegedly organized girls' massages, aka rapes; Nadia Marcinkova, the billionaire's on-again, off-again Slovakian girlfriend; and Lesley Groff, his longtime executive assistant. Kel-len, through her spokesperson, has said that she, too, was a vic-tim; that victimhood, however, did not stop her from destroying me and scores of others. Similarly, Marcinkova's lawyers have said she is a victim who "is and has been severely traumatized."

Groff has admitted through her attorney that she made appointments for Jeffrey, but she says she "did not commit any misconduct at any time." Still, it seems to me that she would've had to at least *suspect* impropriety, given how central I witnessed her to be in Jeffrey's daily operation. In a 2005 *New York Times* piece, "Working for Top Bosses on Wall St. Has Its Perks," she said this of Jeffrey: "I know what he is thinking and I know when I need to be fast. It's a nice roll we are on." In that article, Jeffrey said he paid Groff and his other assistants more than two hundred thousand dollars annually and gifted Groff with a Benz and a nanny. "They are an extension of my brain," he noted. Yet Jeffrey's second brains have come down with amnesia. Perks, it appears, can purchase silence.

Unnamed in the plea deal yet towering amid the sisterhood of conspirators: Madam Maxwell, the lead orchestrator of the vast and venomous scheme. The Oxford-educated blueblood weaned and reared on elitist condescension. The aristocratic pimp who so cavalierly discarded "these girls" as human rubbish.

4

The Reset

My lids slid shut in a Jo'burg hospital in December 1999. Af-ter I had downed that palm full of pills, my mother rushed me there for a dose of activated charcoal, a medicine used to in-duce vomiting. One week later, on Christmas Eve, I found myself in the Scottish Highlands. Mum has never forgiven me for what happened next.

Before my suicide attempt, our holiday trip to see Auntie Wendy and Uncle Derek had already been on the books. My mother ar-ranged for my early release so that we could still make our flight there. When we arrived in Scotland, my auntie took one look at me, black vomit still under my nails and half unconscious on her sofa, and she knew she had to step up. *At last, a lifeline.*

Out of Mum's earshot and later to her rage, I quietly begged my aunt and uncle to let me come live with them and their chil-dren, my cousins. In hushed tones after Mum had retired to bed, I made my case with a quivering voice. "If I go back to Jo'burg," I said, "I will die." That was no hyperbole. I had begged my father to allow me to move to Cape Town, but he and my stepmother flatly refused. My aunt and uncle sensed my despair and agreed to take me in. Auntie Wendy, who had also been cut out of her father's wealth, nonetheless pleaded for his assistance. He purchased my ticket to return to Scotland, a gift meant more to spite Mum than to help me. We breathed not a word to my mother. Back in Jo'burg that January, I repacked my bags before revealing my plan.

Fire erupted. How could her sister and father not have consulted her, Mum roared. How could I, her only daughter, be so cruel as to abandon her? How could I move six thousand miles away from her and James, with no plan of ever returning? In place of answers to douse her wrath, I spoke a resolve that stoked it. I could no longer be my mother's savior and my father's forgotten. I would not survive in a house, a society, where wine flowed strong as the Nile and men raped me without fear of reprisal. This stallion had to run for her life. With Mum's heart in her throat and bitterness coursing through her, she saw me off to my new forever. I gave her no other option.

I landed in a culture shock. My relatives lived in a pocket-sized village called Boat of Garten, population under seven hundred. Blink while eyeing a map and you'll miss it. It's two and a half hours by car from Edinburgh, the capital, and three or so from Glasgow, the thriving cultural center. A visit to the area's heather-clad hills would charm most city dwellers; a relocation there might put them to sleep. Out with the sweltering summers in the diverse Rainbow Nation; in with lily-white faces and October snow to match. I traded the pulsating Jo'burg for an upstairs guest room overlooking a bucolic sheep field. With one glance around the village square, I knew my social calendar had been severely curtailed. I felt as if I'd been dropped into an Old World Gaelic folktale.

The reset was precisely what I needed. The move out of mayhem and into a Celtic Mayberry steadied my stance and altered my trajectory. I still bless my aunt and uncle for intervening, and especially my cousin Douglas for embracing me. Of the family's six children, he and Shona were the two still living at home. Shona is a few years older than me; Douglas is one year younger. In place of sneaking my way into discotheques, I now huddled with the family to play Trivial Pursuit or traveled to Douglas's games (he's brilliant at basketball). And rather than traipsing through Jo'burg while puffing a cig, I had my nose in a book and my palm on a Hoover, completing my share of the chores. We'd often go on strolls through the surrounding lush forests, drink in the stillness, marvel at the deer, deepen our communion with creation. My bedtime was 10 p.m. sharp, my body in full withdrawal. I'd arrived there, at the ripe old age of fifteen, perched on the brink of alcoholism. My relatives wouldn't tolerate insolence, much less a flask of brandy in my bag. My auntie heaped affection on me, just as Mum always had, with hugs and home-cooked meals, plus trips to the hairdresser and dermatologist (I had horrible acne then; my smoking and swigging worsened it). Every Christmas, I awakened to a stocking on my bed, same as the other children. Overall, and by a mile, my three and a half years with the Everest family were among my most stable.

Our existence was more pauper-like than princely. Sans the benefit of Grandpa's plentiful pounds, my aunt held down a job as a teaching assistant, tutoring children with autism and Down syndrome. She also lent her talents to FACES, the Family Association for Children with Extra Special Needs. My uncle, an enterprising Italian, cobbled together income from various jobs, not all of which I can recall. At one point, he oversaw a gardening center; at all times, he stayed productive. They were far from wealthy and hence industrious. I worked as well, because though Mum sent money regularly, I was expected to cover my incidentals: driving lessons, makeup, some clothing. At sixteen, I began waitressing at a restaurant in a lovely log cabin. I did a double shift on either Saturdays or Sundays. On Wednesdays, once my algebra was finished, I accompanied my aunt to the charity. Then and on some weekends, I made good money chaperoning the children on outings to give their parents respite. The fulfillment in lifting others enlivened me more than it did them.

My grades rocketed north, thanks to strict boundaries enforced. I went from Ds and Fs to a row of Bs, each standing tall and proud. My grandfather, cantankerous as he was, came through for me academically. He arranged for my enrollment at Grantown Grammar, a great secondary school a scenic fifteen-minute drive away. Douglas was my classmate. I entered halfway through what's known there as S3—third year—the equivalent of a sophomore in a US high school. We rode in daily with my dear auntie, who worked at the affiliated primary school. I traveled home by bus, through glens and moorlands adorning the countryside, areas more remote than even ours. Aboard that bus, I basked in nature's presence, just as I had on a Greyhound years earlier.

At school, I was mostly the odd girl out. In a region as close-knit as the Highlands, students form their cliques during their earliest years in the classroom. Also, I hailed from another planet. My peers assumed that growing up in South Africa had made me racist, given what they'd read about the cruelties of apartheid. As wrongheaded as that notion is, I didn't try to correct it, nor did I point out the hypocrisy in their view. (The Scots and the English have been locked in a centuries-long conflict over religion and land. The dispute may not involve skin color, but it has bred the same hatred exhibited in my homeland and nations the world over throughout history. No country, community, or individual is immune to hostility and barbarism; the potential for it is stitched into humanity's DNA. Ordinary people can be conditioned to commit monstrous deeds.) Still, rather than disputing my classmates' claims, I trained my gaze on my English assignments and befriended the few who welcomed me. A pair of Fionas—Smith and Reed—as well as one delightful Gemma Robertson became my center of gravity. I also had swimming. I took to the pool again and shattered more records, sailed and beamed my way to bliss.

My outsider status with my classmates made me an insider with teachers. I would hover near their lounge and often join them for tea and biscuits, sopping up their honey, relishing their conversations. They could sense, I'm sure, my hunger for affirmation, as well as my difficult past. They encouraged and admonished me in equal measures, celebrated my every progress and tutored me after classes. I blossomed, academically and emotionally, beneath their tender palms.

Father John, an ebullient young priest, likewise nurtured me. I began my own spiritual journey at an early age, yet to my annoyance, Mum and Dad hadn't had me christened. James's infant head was sprinkled, but for reasons unclear to me, I missed out on the holy trickle. Auntie's face brightened at my desire to explore my faith. She and my uncle, longtime Catholics, connected me with their clergyman, Father John, who led me through catechism. Once a week, our family gathered over supper— say, chicken Kiev and mash, and one of my auntie's delectable trifles—and then the priest and I lingered at the table. *What is the Blessed Trinity? Who is God? Why had He seemingly punished me by allowing my innocence to be stolen? Would I ever be whole again in His eyes?* Father John, cheeks raised and eyes dancing, gave thoughtful replies I ponder to this moment. I didn't always understand the nuances of scripture, but I felt sure of a connection to God, the Force beyond humanity. My yearlong studies culminated with my conversion and baptism, a ceremonial cleansing of my past sins and a sense of peace and pardon. Following a special Holy Communion, the parishioners each presented me with a handmade gift, mirroring the unearned merit the Creator shows me still.

As my faith became my rock, my grandpa remained my conundrum. That man was a study in contrasts, one moment stolid, the next, verklempt. I'm fortunate he was keen on me, or as fond as his stoicism would allow him to express. His soft spot at times wedged a space between me and the Everest family (as in the Christmas he bought me a glistening Gaelic bracelet, while giving my poor auntie some antiwrinkle cream. . . . He could be a real prick). My grandfather, I surmised, frowned on my aunt because she, like my mum, hadn't married a titled man to continue her place in the peerage. Despite her father's dismissal, Auntie Wendy longed to be close with her father, increasingly so as time went on. She also wanted her children to know the Macpherson patriarch.

My arrival cracked open the door for reunion. One weekend a month, we visited Grandpa's splendorous Kyllachy House, twenty-five miles northwest of our village. The Victorian estate, set on almost two thousand acres, was and still is a majesty to behold (it has since been converted into a luxury sporting lodge.) The immaculately kept lawns stretched into infinity, with vast shooting ranges and salmon and trout fishing in the Upper Findhorn river. Squirrels scurried about; eagles and pheasants flapped their greetings. Beyond the majestic doors of the main house, horned stag and deer heads—Grandpa's hunting prizes—stared down at us from high walls. We gathered for brunch at exquisite place settings, with thistle and azalea brimming from crystal vases. Grandpa insisted on irreproachable etiquette. I once poured wine incorrectly and he gently chastised me; another time, when I walked the wrong way around the dining table, he whispered, "Sarah, that's not how we do it," and nodded me in the opposite direction. After a scrumptious meal of fresh fish, Douglas and I scampered off for tennis while the grownups blathered on about heaven knows what. Auntie treasured time with her father, better scarce than never. Kyllachy is as close to an earthly paradise as I have ever come.

I bonded with Grandpa in the garden. We'd wander there, just the two of us, and spend hours amid the rows of beautiful orchids: purple, canary, butterfly, spotted. As he weeded, I prattled on about school and swimming and the life I'd left behind. For every hundred words I spoke, he uttered the occasional, "Yes, dear," a smile showcasing his affection. Yet when I leaned into that warmth, sat near him on the sofa or tried to hug him, he tensed up, as if to control a dam of emotion he'd stored inside for decades. None of us should be defined by a single face, by the mask we most often display. It conceals a series of disparate others, those just as much who we are. My grandfather could be cruel and kind, heartless and courteous. He was, as we all are, a breathing contradiction.

Our relationship ended abruptly in 2001. I was seventeen that summer. Jennifer Margaret Macpherson, my grandpa's daughter with his second wife, was engaged. She and her then fiancé, Andrew Linehan, hosted a lavish wedding. The bride's and groom's families were, per the custom, seated up front. The Everests and I, however, were relegated to the rear and stood for the entire ceremony. No pew had been reserved. At the reception, my auntie, reared in a snobbery she hadn't entirely set aside, burst a blood vessel when she discovered she was seated next to the *gardener*! It was an aristocratic slap in the face, a demonstration of her father's scorn. She felt as sidelined as she'd been in childhood. We left halfway through the festivities as my auntie wept. When it's hysterical, as they say, it's historical. Her old wound had been ripped open.

That was the last time I saw my grandfather. My auntie was so crushed that, to my disappointment, our brunches ended. Just as I was getting to know my grandpa, settling into what I had hoped would be an ever-blossoming friendship, our connection was severed. Out of respect for my aunt, who'd opened her home and heart to me, I stopped all communication with Grandpa. Also, it wasn't as if I could just pick up the phone and say, "Yo, Gramps, I'm coming to see you!" I had no car and, above all, no interest in slathering salt on my auntie's sore spot.

The bell tolled for my grandfather in 2008, when he succumbed to pneumonia. He had been ill for years with various ailments. As he lay suffering, his wife looked after his health and wealth. Following his death, my grandfather's heir, the Honorable James Anthony, took his new place in the peerage amid a quake. He had married Kitty Zetenyi Budai of Budapest, Hungary, a choice that sent shockwaves through a family not keen on outsiders. Still, the 3rd Baron of Drumochter received his title and his due. By then, I'd long left the heavenly Kyllachy and entered a private hell.

Upon my grandfather's passing, James and I discovered that, since our births, Grandpa been setting aside money in a trust fund to finance our education. Those funds magically vanished after he died. In place of my grandfather's lifetime of savings for us, my brother and I each received two hundred pounds—about $275. I was grateful for the pittance even as I resented the apparent thievery. James ripped up his check and burned the pieces.

When I fled Jo'burg, Mum experienced a reset of her own. Her life collapsed into shambles, similar to how Granny's had after Tommy's accident. She had a full nervous breakdown. Her addiction grabbed hold of her throat and would not stop squeezing. The business, already teetering on a cliff edge, fell off and exploded. James, who'd already finished high school, struggled to help Mum rebound. Yet our mother's heartache proved impossible to quell. She believed that she'd failed in the most grievous of ways, broken the parental oath to protect one's babe. She also railed against my auntie and grandfather for having "kidnapped" me, as she understandably saw it. She has never gotten over the agony. I mourn with her as I maintain my stance. If I had to do it all over, I'd make the same decision, because if this life is anything, it is a quest to survive. I chose to live. I have compassion for the fifteen-year-old girl who had to make such a wrenching exit.

Mum and I rarely spoke during my first year in Scotland. When we did, she vacillated between shouts and sobs, blaming and regretting. After losing her business, she ended up homeless. She reconnected with an old classmate, Annie, who agreed to let her stay with her and her husband in the UK, until she could find a job. So in 2001, Mum packed the remaining shards of her life and relocated to Petersfield, sixty miles outside London. Jack, the landscape architect she'd broken up with, had also moved to southern England, which increased the move's appeal. Despite their toxic union, or maybe because of it, Mum was still in love with him. She also yearned for us to be closer. Once she got settled, I traveled to see her occasionally. However, my school and work schedules—and my desire to stay on the page I had turned, rather than flipping back to bedlam—kept daylight between us. Dad and I were in touch. Our geographic distance paralleled our long-standing emotional one. James, who remained in Jo'burg for university, held down two gigs to pay his way. He was on his own. I would be soon.

My final year of high school was a welcome whirlwind. I was

chosen as Head Girl, an honor in recognition of one's leadership and service, the highest award a student can receive. In a childhood abounding with feelings of deep shame, the designation lifted my chin. It also fueled my fervency for outreach. On National Poetry Day, I rallied my classmates to share sonnets with the elderly in care homes. I raised a thousand pounds for the special needs children of FACES by completing a parachute jump. As I searched for ways to serve, I held fast to the words of Mother Teresa. "If you can't feed a hundred people," she said, "then feed just one." I live by that credo.

My parachute leap spawned other adventures. I completed the Duke of Edinburgh's Award, the program Prince Philip pioneered to inspire volunteering, sport, social skills, and expedition. For my sport I naturally chose swimming, and also open-boat canoeing. I set out on the River Spey with my friend Fiona Smith and camped under the stars at stops along the journey. On the water, with tides swaying us here and yonder, I felt wholly at one with Mother Nature. I have never forgotten my senior year, that rapturous denouement. When I graduated in summer 2003, I did so with a full heart.

I knew I would attend college. In my mother's day, women went to the wedding chapel rather than to university. I wanted different. I had navigated a girlhood screaming "Loser!" at me from all directions, and I felt determined to change the refrain. College would be my path to redemption, a way to blot out my past blemishes and garner my family's admiration. My grandfather respected education. My dad lit up at its mention. And once I earned a diploma, that accomplishment could never be seized like my virginity had been years earlier. I enrolled at Queen Margaret University in Edinburgh and deferred my spot during gap year, a sabbatical common in Europe. Though I didn't have the money to begin, I now wish I'd gone straight away.

Mum pleaded for me to come to Petersfield so we could rekindle our relationship. She had her own place by then, on the outskirts of town. Her tearful request melted me, mostly because I missed her, loved her, wanted to be near her again. I was also grappling with a fresh round of guilt over my decision to leave Jo'burg. You can be certain that you've made the right choice yet regret its impact on others. My escape saved my life but torpedoed Mum's. I hope I'm never so callous that a fervent appeal doesn't stir me. Still, what I experienced in England hurled me down a steep slippery slope.

Mum's world had unraveled. She'd landed a job in advertising but soon lost her license because of drunk driving. That left her reliant on long bus trips to get to work, as well as to run even small errands. Her hot-and-cold romance with Jack had hit an icy patch, so he was mostly out of the picture. Mom's liquor became her lover, the relationship she held in her bosom. I once awakened to a trail of blood along our hallway. My mother had staggered home at 2 a.m. and couldn't find her gate key. She scaled the iron gate, pierced her nose on a spike, and dripped beads of scarlet all the way to her bedroom. When the blackout wore off, she had no memory of the evening. She had already been banned from local pubs—drinking and rowing and dancing arm in arm—yet she'd somehow found her way to a party. I write this without the slightest hint of sanctimony, but rather with great sorrow. My mother was sick. Addiction is as much an illness as cancer is. I myself have struggled to break free from alcohol's iron grip, so I understand the difficulty. My mother needed my helping hand, not my raised brow. That is why I returned to Petersfield. And that's why I felt desperate enough to do what I did next.

I had started waitressing. I worked six days a week to feverishly save shillings for college. Then Mum lost her job, and I had to cover our rent, reprising my role as caretaker. I could hardly keep the lights on, even when I added a seventh day to my schedule. I earned minimum wage (£4.20 then, or $7), plus good tips if I was fortunate, a luck that fluctuated. I had heard a woman mention that she made twenty pounds an hour as an exotic dancer—quadruple my salary for what sounded like a quarter of the work. In one night, she raked in nearly two hundred pounds (about $275). That planted a seed. I mulled the notion for weeks. I had been assaulted so much by then that the idea of baring myself didn't faze me. The first rape, the one in my own bed, had not only stolen my innocence. It had also prematurely awakened my sexual awareness, robbed me of the natural reticence most children have, made me feel permanently tainted. Still, I wasn't quite comfortable with the thought of dancing. Even a broken spirit can whisper the truth mine did: *you're better than this*. That inkling won out, and I went back to taking food orders.

And then I came up short on rent. Jack lent us money one month. My auntie and uncle, who were already stretching their income, couldn't help. Calling my grandfather was out of the question. By this time, his wife, who had never shown kindness for me or Mum, seemed to be gripping the Macpherson purse strings. Also, I hadn't spoken to Grandpa since the wedding fiasco two years earlier. My father had no cash to spare. So I took on double shifts, even searched for side gigs. I was terrified we'd end up homeless, as Mum had twice before. I was also beyond exhausted, a zombie lumbering from work to home and back again, with lids threatening to slam shut. I turned to dancing as a final resort.

I contacted a gentleman's club in London, a well-established chain with strict rules for patrons. No kissing. No fondling. No touching of any kind. If men solicited phone numbers, or failed to keep six feet away from dancers, they were forced to leave. I became one of about fifty young women, many as forlorn as I, swiveling their hips to the tune of survival. One girl I befriended was a professional dancer who had trained in the fine arts. She was petite, with long black hair and kind eyes. When she fell on hard times, she used her day-job talent to get back on her feet. She'd been renting a room in a shanty in a seamy area. Courtesy of her club income, she was able to get her own studio in a good neighborhood. She was the nicest girl, someone you might smile at on the street. Her work in the club was a stop-gap measure, not a long-term career. There were other sorts as well, dancers who had carved out a lavish lifestyle, rolled up in Porsches, came to work high as a kite to numb what can only be called a soul-destroying act. Never once did I meet a dancer who had grown up dreaming she'd one day shimmy on a pole.

My comrades became my competitors once on the floor. The evening began with us parading through the club in high wedge heels and sheer evening gowns. The men, the wolves—husbands, fathers, alphas, betas—howled from the sidelines. Round Two's clothing change involved a corset and a bow tie. Later, some of us took to the poles, while others danced on the stage. Each woman rotated from space to space, including into private booths monitored by guards. Whoever performed best took home the largest bounty, and I can assure you that wasn't moi. God gave me a talent for swimming but overlooked me in the rhythm department. I danced like a complete lunatic. I was also flat-chested, as nearly any woman would appear beside my breast-enhanced counterparts. More men wanted to take me home than watch me twirl (I gave a few beggars my number, but we never hooked up). Even on a slow week, and even after handing over the club's cut, I cleared one thousand pounds ($1,400)—enough for rent and meals. Mum knew I was performing but turned two blind eyes. I had danced her into solvency and silence.

And yet the job exacted a high toll. I had convinced myself I'd be cool with the exposure, even shrugged it off in the beginning. I thought, *If men are just going to rape me with their drooling, their cat-calling, their back-seat thrusting, then why shouldn't I be paid for it?* I silenced my inner voice, the nagging awareness that I had unwittingly become my own assailant. A predator needn't prowl in the shadows. I presented myself as prey, a girl prepared to be ogled and slaughtered. Over years I'd absorbed my own sense of deep inadequacy, behaved in alignment with that feeling. The pay, lucrative as it was, could not offset the loss of self-respect. For every pound earned, my honor slipped away in greater measure. The work filled my coffers while further contaminating my spirit. The pungent odor, the silent contempt I held for myself, permeated my pores. I bathed and cleansed, prayed and purified, yet the smell, the disrespect, lingered ever after. No triumph in the pool, no appointment as Head Girl, could overpower that stench.

Just as there are certain rape victims most likely to be believed, there are others discredited with a glance. Exotic dancers. Escorts. Streetwalkers. Addicts. The homeless and the marginalized. Before such a woman can even speak, her value has been disregarded. She is no longer human in the eyes of most. She is "other." She is filthy. She is inebriated. She is loathsome and disposable, judgments she heaps on herself long before society nods in agreement. The othering, the dismissal of her intrinsic worth, needn't be articulated. It's evident in the hastily averted eyes of strangers, in their groans and grimaces as she walks by, in the way a room clears when she enters. Those who pass her glimpse one moment in her story, a frightful coda, with no awareness of the miseries preceding it. Life conditioned me as well to look askance at the stigmatized. And then, in despair, I became one.

The world thumbs its nose at so-called strippers and harlots, terms reeking of disdain. I have banned the word *prostitute* from my vocabulary and replaced it with a far more accurate characterization—survival sex worker. When I cross paths with these brave women, I now see children once barbarized, sufferers turning their horror on themselves, wielding the knife that first mutilated them. The world uses labels like *whore* and *dopehead* to expel some from the human family. I regard them as the walking wounded, those who have stumbled into a Sophie's choice, a decision between two equally horrible heartaches. They're not the lepers many view them as. They are people, graced by the Almighty with incalculable esteem, forced to trade their pride for a meal and a bed. They are me. They are you. They are us.

5

Edinburgh

I received a call from Auntie Wendy the summer I turned twenty-one. The conversation started with bewildered stammering. It ended in loud wails.

"Sarah, are you working in a hotel now?" my aunt asked.

Long pause. "I mean . . . um . . . I don't know . . . why do you ask?" I stuttered.

"One of your cousin's friends saw you leaving a hotel in Edinburgh last evening."

I pressed the receiver into my ear. "That must've been someone else," I said with a quiver in my voice. "I haven't . . . uh, no . . . I'm not sure what you're talking about."

Silence. "Are you certain?" she asked. "Because someone else also mentioned seeing you there two weeks ago."

I lost it. A tidal wave of tears streamed down my face as I set aside the phone. I could hear my auntie repeating, "Are you still there?" as I doubled over onto my couch. My secret had somehow been discovered. There was little else to talk about.

A year earlier, in autumn 2004, I had entered Queen Margaret University. Mum had rebounded in Petersfield, with a job,
a restored driver's license, and the financial cushion I'd left for
her. College felt like my second chance, or third, if you count
my Jo'burg escape. My dancing days were behind me. My future
shone so brightly it burned my eyes.

My aunt and uncle dropped me off at my residence hall. The
parting was a wee bit uncomfortable. My classmates' parents lingered in the lobby, bidding farewell with dew on their lids, while
two emotions surged through me. The first was deep gratitude
to the Everests for taking me in. The second was trepidation. My
peers, many of whom hailed from nearby Ireland, were entering
a passageway toward final autonomy. Most were leaving home for
the first time. I, full stop, had long been on my own, had lived on
two continents and provided for Mum. So as those around me
swapped promises to write, I awkwardly hugged my relatives and
lurched toward the uncertain. My aunt and uncle had done their
duty. Life was now up to me.

Psychology and sociology were my chosen courses of study.
I had so enjoyed my work with the children's charity in Scotland that I mused over a career in social work. Yet like myriad
freshmen across the globe, I had no concrete idea how I'd end
up using my degree. I just knew I had to have one. A diploma
was my passport to worthiness, with validity stamped on each
page. What matters in my family, above most else, is appearance.
Respectability. Bringing honor to the Macpherson and Ransome
names. I dreamed of returning to South Africa, postgraduation,
and hearing my father say, "Well done, you!" My true major was

exoneration. My hope was that by completing my studies, I'd trade my shame for an enduring pride.

I sensed I was in trouble almost immediately. My taste for alcohol came roaring back during Freshers Week, a liquor-fueled introduction to life in the hangover lane. I hadn't touched alcohol since my withdrawal in Boat of Garten, and only here and there when I started dancing. Sobriety had become a feather in my cap. That feather was soon replaced by a shot glass. Tequila shots flowed generously. In the dorms. At parties. All over the campus and city. I drank myself insane, guzzled cider by day and hard liquor by night. At class time, I was totally hammer-fucked; at my waitressing job, I could hardly stand upright. While my schoolmates were away during holidays, reconnecting with the families who mailed them care packages, I was passed out on my dorm-room floor, or else waking up next to yet another boy I didn't recognize. Now and again my relatives rang me, and I assured them all was fine. It wasn't. At the time I thought my carousing was just a raucous celebration, happy independence day to me. In hindsight, I see I was panicked about my studies and near certain I'd fail at my first big test of young adulthood. Also, inside this stallion lives a shy girl, a bit of an introvert. I drank to ease my social anxiety. The more I imbibed, the more effervescent I felt.

For a boozer who barhopped till sunup, I did surprisingly well the first semester, earning more Bs than Ds. Among my whiny classmates who constantly complained of homesickness, I found two mature friends. Cara, Chrissy, and I became so tight that we decided to move off campus together. Dormitory life was not for me. For one thing, I'm not keen on sharing a kitchen with fifty hall mates (my groceries got swiped from the fridge). For another, let's just say I insist on a pristine sink and shower. So, during the spring term of our freshman year, the three of us got a place near the university, a twenty-minute bus ride away. Tuition is covered for EU residents enrolled in Scotland's undergraduate programs. Room, board, books, and expenses, however, were my responsibility. I had blown through a lot of cash during my months-long Oktoberfest. Still, I had enough for my share of the security deposit and rent.

At least initially. I faithfully paid my bills for a few months, but by midspring 2005, I was coming up short. I took on more waitressing shifts. My grades suffered accordingly. I scraped by with help from my housemates, who lent me money and also bought me groceries. It pained me that I couldn't pay my way, thus prompting the cycle of addiction: Experience any uncomfortable emotion. Binge drink to deaden it. Exacerbate your crisis. Wash, rinse, repeat. When I had arrived in Scotland at age fifteen, I'd stood in addiction's foyer. In college, I became a full-fledged alcoholic, in the tradition of Granny and Mum. I am not just my mother's daughter. I am my mum.

Credit cards became my buoy. I stayed afloat by charging everything that summer: rent (a larger share since my housemates had traveled home to be with their families for the break), plus food, toiletries, bus fare, cell phone. I took out a student loan and signed up for credit cards. Mum was faring better but still could not help me, so Jack, her on-again, off-again beau, once wired me six hundred pounds (about $700). That staved off homelessness for a time. My brother sympathized, but as a broke student supporting himself, he couldn't lend a hand. My father's business was then flailing, so he was unable to assist. My aunt and uncle were in no position to help, beyond how they so generously already had in relocating me to Scotland. Meanwhile, my phone was lighting up with a tempting solution.

My former patrons at the gentlemen's club in London were texting me with offers. "If I can see you for one hour," an executive wrote, "I'll pay you a thousand Pounds." My number had apparently been passed around, because men I hadn't met were requesting my services. I fought with myself for a few weeks. *Please don't go back down that road, Sarah*, I told myself. *Just stay the course.* I did for a time. But that voice grew dimmer as my bills stacked up. Cara and Chrissy loaned me more money, but they couldn't carry me indefinitely. Also, word had gotten out that I was quick to raise my hemline. A visit to campus became a walk of shame, complete with whispers when I entered the Student Union building. So partway through my autumn 2005 semester, I stepped away from my studies. I promised myself I'd return. I just needed to shore up my savings and pay my housemates back. By the time I dropped out of university, I'd maxed out four credit cards and owed twelve thousand pounds—just over sixteen thousand dollars. When I told my father I'd disenrolled, he sighed and said, "This will be the biggest mistake of your life." Though saddened by his lack of contribution, some part of me believed him.

I stayed in the apartment and interviewed for jobs all over the city, something that paid better than restaurant work. I submitted my résumé for a job as a recruitment agent at headhunting firms that curate candidates. I had heard such agents earned good money, and a degree was not always necessary for landing the position. I applied all over the city to no avail, so I continued waiting tables. At this point, earning an income was about restoring calm. Creditors were harassing me at all hours because I'd fallen way behind on even minimum payments. The lion's share of my tip money went to Visa. Another portion went to the four banks I'd borrowed from. And all the while the texts continued, from men who sweetened their offers. My old rationale boomeranged back. *You're sleeping around Edinburgh anyway*, I thought. *You might as well be paid for it.* Once you've bared your bosom in exotic dancing, you're just a half step away from going all the way. Stripping is escorting's gateway drug. So with my resources dwindling and my rent in arrears, I walked through that door. How I wish I could go back and slam it shut.

I told neither of my housemates I was escorting. Both, however, sleuthed it out. One shunned me. The other showed me a warmth I've never forgotten. Yet it was soon apparent that I needed my own place. So I signed on with a local escort agency and worked for a few weeks. I also traveled, by train, three hours down to London to meet with clients who gladly covered my transportation costs. I got my own apartment elsewhere in Edinburgh, and from then on, I saw two to three men weekly. Some were married, in strained relationships. All were wealthy professionals, the clientele the agency specialized in. A few did not want intercourse, just two hours of companionship, or sometimes just to kiss and cuddle. The irony is that my clients treated me with greater respect than many men I had met in bars and gone on dates with. Still, no matter how much deference a man shows, sharing intimacy with a stranger hurls a dagger at the soul. I drank to stem the bleeding.

Most men met me in hotel rooms around Edinburgh. That was a mistake. Scotland's capital is relatively small, and word spreads like clotted cream on scones fresh out of the oven. My cousin Douglas was enrolled at Edinburgh Napier University, just a few miles from my apartment. One of his classmates worked part-time at a hotel and saw me enter and go up to a room. Another evening I had been spotted walking in with a man who appeared to be twice my age. You needn't be a Scotland Yard detective to piece together the puzzle. My cousin, humiliated by the sightings, mentioned them to his family. My auntie and uncle's eldest son, Graham, a policeman in Glasgow at the time, did a brief under-cover investigation on me. He discovered that I had signed up with an escort service. Soon after, my auntie called me.

The fallout was massive. I understand in retrospect why Douglas told his parents about my covert life, but at the time, brimstone coursed through my veins. The entire family was horrified that I had resorted to selling my body, bringing disgrace to the tribe. That did not stun me. What shook me to my core was how little they seemed to care about how I'd ended up escorting. I had no money. No parents who could cushion my fall. No trust fund, no word from a wealthy grandfather who had long since moved on from our garden heart-to-hearts. They felt mortified. I felt judged. My auntie demanded I stop work immediately. I slammed down the phone and sobbed. I wasn't proud of my escorting. I'm still not. But there's a reason prostitution is dubbed the world's oldest profession. It's what generations of women have had to do in order to survive.

Maya Angelou, the great poet and writer once muted by childhood rape, titled her first memoir *I Know Why the Caged Bird Sings*. That bird trills its lament, I've come to feel, because it is parched and defeated. Floundering financially while Grandpa boasted of millions felt like staring, dehydrated, at a creek. I could see the fresh water, hear its torrents rush. I yearned for a sip, prayed the brook would flow my way. But because of a barrier between me and the stream, I could not reach it, drink it, save myself. It would have been less dispiriting had I never witnessed what would not quench my thirst.

My explosion with the Everests wrecked our relationship. We haven't been close since. I don't know if my auntie ever mentioned my escorting to my mother, but I told her myself. The disappointment in her voice broke my heart. We never spoke about it again. Perhaps she coped by pretending it hadn't happened, that I'd never been desperate enough to make such a choice. In The Story of my ancestry, that thread line is not new. For years between my mother and me, as it had been with her and her mother, much remained unspoken—a silence both deafening and destructive.

I had been escorting for only a short time when I crossed paths with Rick. It was around autumn 2005. My girlfriend Lynn and a few others we knew went out for drinks one evening. Rick was seated at the bar. He approached, offered to buy me a cocktail, and I was besotted from that moment. He was in his midthirties. I was then twenty-one. His face appeared sculpted from smooth, rich marble: square jawline, broad smile, unruly short curls falling onto his wide forehead. A rocker type, he exuded charisma, a magnetism that thrilled me. We traded a list of music genre favorites, Metallica, beat, house. He also played the electric guitar, my kind of masculine for sure. We got so caught up in talk of bands and artists that I neglected to ask his profession. Toward evening's end he invited Lynn, me, and the others to his place. When we drove up, I thought, *Who the hell is this guy?*

His home was palatial, a four-level house in one of Edinburgh's toniest neighborhoods. He was an entrepreneur who had launched a global software company, one successful enough to land him in this swank mansion. The top floor housed a soundproof music room, with drums, guitars, pianos. The other floors were lavishly appointed, with labyrinthine halls leading from one door to another. I didn't stay long because I developed a (tequila) migraine, but he asked for my number and rang me the next day. "I want to take you out on a *real* first date," he gushed. His words wafted straight toward my Father Wound. "Sure," I chirped like a giggling schoolgirl. The next week he drove me to the Witchery, a romantic restaurant in one of the city's most affluent areas. If I had been infatuated on night one, I was picking my bridesmaid colors by the second. I weep for the girl I was then. It took so little, the smallest hint of fondness, for me to fall not in love but in longing. I ached for a man's care in the abyss carved out by my father.

The spoiling carried on. I didn't mention my escorting to Rick and actually began phasing out of it. I hadn't wanted to enter that world in the first place, and with an affluent suitor in the picture, I had no interest in continuing. Around that time, I finally got a job at a recruitment agency and also landed freelance modeling work. Men often asked me whether I had ever modeled. While blushing at the suggestion, I took it as a sign of my aptitude. On a whim, I signed up for a bikini competition at a bar. Surprisingly, given my novice status at sashaying, I won. First prize was a modeling contract with a local agency. I did a couple of runway gigs. Though I'm five foot nine, I've never been rail-thin enough to make it on the catwalk. I weighed 65 kilograms then, about 146 pounds—slender, but no Kate Moss. Most of my work was commercial, posing for regional print publications. With income from modeling and my job in recruiting, I was able to stop escorting.

I kept my small apartment but spent the bulk of my time at Rick's place. The wine was ubiquitous, the drugs abundant. Rick, a recreational cocaine user, introduced me to a new way to numb. We snorted and laughed and made love in the shadows, went to sleep stoned and woke up enraptured, even if hungover. I hadn't had a proper beau in high school. My aunt and uncle wouldn't have allowed it. I did plenty of swiping right in college, but those connections, mostly hookups, felt fleeting and hollow. Rick is the first man I had ever given my heart to, if such a reckless offering can be called a gift.

We'd been dating for about three months when I told Rick about my dancing and escorting. I didn't initially think I'd ever disclose my twin shames, but I naively believed that we were on the path to marriage. I couldn't live with an immense lie between us, a falsehood hindering intimacy. "That explains a lot," he said unflinchingly after hearing my account. I wasn't quite sure what he meant. I only know that, after that conversation, the energy between us permanently changed. He thanked me for my candor and reassured me he saw me no differently. His actions shouted otherwise.

Our intercourse tilted toward the pornographic. He had a warped sexuality and forced me to participate in his perverted fantasies. He once wrapped me entirely in cling film so I was helpless to move, leaving an opening at my rear so he could sodomize me. Another time, with awareness of my past, he made me dress up as a hooker as part of a cruel role-play. When I entered the room, he threw pound notes at me. He then flung me on the bed and raped me. The more he violated me, the more tightly I held on to him. Abuse, however torturous, meant I was visible, worthy of at least reprehensible regard.

Our six-month romance went up in flames when I discovered he was cheating—a betrayal he'd accused me of. He who protests the loudest, it has been said, is often the guiltiest. A dreadful scene one morning seemed proof of that truism. I came downstairs and found Rick naked in the middle of his living floor, making out with two nude women I didn't know. He'd been gaslighting me for months, insisting that I, not he, was stepping out on our relationship. Yet there he lay, cradled by irrefutable evidence of his own disloyalty.

Chernobyl ensued. Soon after—because despite that flagrant violation, my abhorrence for myself compelled me back to him—I spotted Rick with a brunette. He had told me he was leaving town, so imagine the WTF on my face when he sped by my bus stop with that girl in his car. There I stood, waiting for public transportation, while he chauffeured this model type around. I confronted him, her, myself. As messed up in the head as I was then, I would not tolerate infidelity. My grandfather had been unfaithful. My dad had done the same. I refused to be with a serial philanderer. I left Rick that week, though I'm loath to admit that, deep down, I was still in love with him. Nearly a decade would pass before I fully reckoned with my heartache over that split.

Rick wasn't done torturing me. He stalked me for weeks after our breakup, randomly turning up at my home and workplace. It frightened and infuriated me, even as it made me secretly ask myself, *Should I give it one more try?* His remorseless womanizing, however, strengthened my resolve. I needed another reset, a new beginning someplace far away, in a city where a dark memory did not haunt me on every corner, not to mention an ex intent on harassment.

I had never visited New York City but had dreamed of living in the land of haute couture. Fashion is one of my life's great loves, ever since those years when I lay gawking at my mum, the consummate fashionista, who worked her magic with a few well-placed accessories. My modeling work, which brought me up close to racks of high-end designs, deepened my love for all things Fifth Avenue. I knew I had no future on the runway. I mused about breaking into design. I also longed to re-enroll in school, increasingly so as I shifted my gaze from Rick to my doleful prospects. My horizon appeared colorless, with no real passion to pursue. My father's voice, his warning that I would regret my choice to leave college, echoed ever louder. Without much thought, a capriciousness bestowed by youth, I booked a ticket to JFK for autumn 2006.

I had just turned twenty-two when I left Edinburgh. I was a broken child in a woman's body. Chronologically, I was of age. Yet emotionally and psychologically, I couldn't have been more lost and vulnerable. I was still that eleven-year-old girl in my bed, clasping my musical teddy bear, weeping in a pool of crimson. As I boarded my flight on that fall evening, I thought my bleakest chapters were behind me. I hadn't yet met Jeffrey and Ghislaine.

Part II

MUTED

The silence was killing me.
And that's all there ever was. Silence.
It was all I knew. Keep quiet. Pretend nothing
had happened, that nothing was wrong.
And look how well that was turning out.

—J. LYNN in *Wait for You*

6

City of Dreams

The *new* in New York lured me to America's shores. The land of dreamers specializes in clean slates. Under Lady Liberty's raised torch, past transgressions are forgotten, future impertinence is allowed. Anonymity is the city's currency, celebrity its hallmark. The island, shrugging its shoulders at all of the above, whispers, "Just do you." I arrived with my focus on fashion, my heart in tatters, and more baggage than I could handle.

I embraced the fresh start. In New York's five boroughs, bursting at the seams with more than eight million souls, no one cared about my history or even my existence. I relished that obscurity as I reeled from the split with Rick. I left Scotland carrying two secret hopes. The first was that, years later, I would run into my ex and show him that I had made something of myself, a middle finger of sorts. He'd then fall to his knees and grovel, pleading, "Sarah, I'm so sorry . . . let's get back together." My second wish was to finally hear from my family, "Look what you've achieved, darling! We're so proud of you." I know now that it was my own respect I most needed to earn.

My Father Wound made my housing arrangements. Just before I left Scotland, I struck up an online chat with Tom, a friendly guy in his forties, who worked as a baseball executive. I hoped that he'd provide a soft place to fall after Rick. I had partied my way through the first two years of my twenties. Amid the revelry, my desire for the Fairy Tale, the happily ever after, nudged me. That's why I was so shattered when Rick and I ended things. He was supposed to be my prince, the one to satisfy the yearning I had long had for my dad's affection. When our romance proved more bruising than magical, I moved on but not forward. I went in search of another man, another father figure, who I thought could fill my void. It's no coincidence that every beau I dated was significantly older than me. I didn't want an equal partnership. I wanted a knight to rescue me, the damsel in distress. I may as well have been walking around with the words *save me* plastered on my forehead. That is the poor-me narrative I was addicted to then and for many years after. To this moment I've struggled to step out of that story line. It pains me now, in my late thirties, to own that. It hurt even more to live it unconsciously.

Tom, I prayed, would be my new hero. When I told him I was moving to his city with nowhere to live, he said I could crash at his Upper East Side apartment. I'm fortunate he turned out to be a sweetheart, not an axe murderer. He also turned out to be not at all my type. He was stout, with a hearty laugh, a chicken-wing-eating, Yankees-cap-wearing dude who took me to a sports bar that first evening. I think we both sensed, from our introductory bear hug, that we were permanently in the friend zone. Still, he was gracious enough to let me stay at his place, and I agreed to pay him rent until I got myself sorted. As nice as he was, his place was disgusting, with dishes stacked in the sink and grime in every corner. That meant I spent a lot of time out exploring.

I came to New York sporting a sleek, black vintage bob, red nails, and red lipstick—very Dita Von Teese, a model, actress, and fashion icon I've long admired. My passport is stamped September 1, 2006, just ahead of Fashion Week. I had grown up watching HBO's *Sex and the City*, starring the Versace-clad, Manolo Blahnik–strutting Carrie Bradshaw, portrayed by the inimitable Sarah Jessica Parker. The fashion capital was her glamorous backdrop. The show, which debuted when I was in high school, became my lens on New York. There I would sit in front of the telly, with a sheep field outside my window in Boat of Garten, watching episode after episode set in a place I could only fantasize about visiting. And now here I was, wandering along Fifth Avenue, staring up at Saks and Bergdorf and Armani, with a sea of yellow taxis honking and weaving alongside me. Forgive my geekiness and this cliché: it was beyond surreal. As my brain absorbed all the sounds and colors, feeling like a small ant among the tall buildings, I could not believe I was in the Big Apple. Everything felt possible.

I mingled constantly from day one. Networking is my superpower, particularly after I've eased my nerves with a glass of wine. I intended to keep myself afloat with freelance modeling (I had only modest savings), so I talked to everyone. Bartenders. Cashiers. Cabbies. I connected with some models, who took me to their agency, and I landed a few gigs. On my second day in the city, I met a gentleman who worked for Ralph Lauren. I don't recall his position, but I hung on to what he told me. "For anyone to take you seriously in fashion here," he said, "you need a degree." He pointed me toward the Fashion Institute of Technology (FIT), the renowned design school along Seventh Avenue at West Twenty-Seventh Street. His mention lit me up. The next day I toured the campus, teeming with wide-eyed creatives, bursting with the vitality of its Chelsea neighborhood. I immediately knew this was the place for me; my goosebumps concurred. I walked from there to Midtown's Garment District, button-and-needle sculpture at its center, and dreamed of my ascent in the design world. This was my yellow brick road to Oz.

That road took a sharp left a few weeks after my arrival. I went out to a nightclub called Quo, a place on Twenty-Third Street and Tenth Avenue in the Meatpacking District. Once there, I drank too much, alternated between the bar and the dance floor, requested the DJ play "Paint It Black," the Rolling Stones hit I love. At midnight, just when I was eyeing the exit, an attractive girl around my age, with dark-brown shoulder-length hair and an easy smile, sidled up to me on the dance floor. Her expression brightened when she spotted me, and by her gaze, I knew she was hitting on me. I'm not bisexual, but I just went with it, shimmied close to her and played along in my black mini dress and matching stilettos. Soon after, we took a spot back at the bar, and in her thick eastern European accent, she told me her name, Natalya Malyshev. She also introduced me to the club's owner, Gary Malhotra, seated next to her.

"What brings you to New York?" she asked. In a drunken soliloquy I poured out my story, from my tragic childhood to the abusive relationship I had escaped, to the squalor of my temporary apartment with Tom. I also asked her a couple of questions—where she was from, why she had moved to Manhattan—but she revealed nothing, just said she was freelancing as a masseuse. After each of my inquiries, she quickly swiveled the spotlight back on me, wanted to know what area of Jo'burg I hailed from, where in Scotland I'd lived, on and on. Gary, a fast-talking, car-salesman type with a goatee and an intense stare, listened in for a while before inviting us to his office in the back. There, he offered us coke. That didn't strike me as odd. Coke seemed to be the way the city's partiers bonded. I had been out every night since my arrival and never once paid for a line. Within a half hour of meeting someone at a bar, I'd hear, "Hey, do you want to do a bump in the restroom?" Strange, yes, but thrilling for me then.

I lost count of how many lines I snorted off the surface of Gary's desk. What I do recall is that Natalya and I, high as Mount Kilimanjaro, made out as the owner watched and eventually joined in. I also remember how elated I was that she and Gary showed such strong interest in me. "You've got the most beautiful eyes," they cooed almost in unison. "You're stunning." I eagerly soaked it up, because that's who I was at the time, a sponge of neediness. As we parted, I gave Natalya my phone number and made my way to Tom's place by taxi. When my lids slid open at noon the next day, I thought, *Did that really happen? Wow. People like me.* After a lifetime of being either bullied or ignored, I felt blessed to be showered with attention.

I wasn't sure I'd ever hear from Natalya. Since I didn't take her number, I had no way of reaching her on my crappy Scottish flip phone, nothing smart about it. Days later, around the time I had decided she'd moved on, she rang me. We shot the breeze for a couple of minutes, with her heaping on more compliments, before she shifted gears. "I know this great guy who's incredibly wealthy," she told me. "He's a philanthropist, and he helps a lot of girls achieve their dreams." She said his name was Jeffrey Epstein, a well-connected businessman who could possibly get me into FIT. I hadn't ever heard of him. "Why would he want to help me?" I asked. "He's just generous," she said. "He does this sort of thing all the time. He's actually helped me financially." I went quiet for a moment as visions of FIT danced in my head. *If she trusts him*, I thought, *he must be all right.* "Do you want to meet him?" she asked. I agreed.

Later that week, she said she'd told Jeffrey about me, and he wanted to connect at a movie theater in Midtown. My heart rate quickened. "Really?" I said. "Yes," she said, "and I'll be there, along with some other girls he's helping." If Jeffrey had asked to meet me alone, I would've bolted for the hills. But because Natalya would be there, and because we'd be meeting in a public place, I saw no reason to recoil. She gave me a few rules. "Don't smoke before-hand," she said. "He hates the smell of cigarettes." She also told me to show up sober, without any hint of liquor on my breath. That seemed bizarre to me, given our drunken debauchery at the club, but I shrugged it off. If this was my path to FIT, I'd happily walk it sans tequila. "In the theater," she said, "you should sit near him. He wants to get to know you." Ahead of the meeting I brushed my teeth like a maniac in an attempt to banish my smoker's breath. I was up to nearly a pack a day.

Natalya and I were in front of the cinema when Jeffrey approached, wearing a red designer coat and a half grin. At his side were about ten girls, maybe a few years younger than me, tall and modelesque, animated and gracious. They each greeted me warmly, welcomed me to the city, embraced me like we were longtime friends. As we exchanged hellos and walked together through the theater, one girl mentioned Jeffrey had helped her line up ballet training. Another said she had broken into modeling, courtesy of Jeffrey's generosity. None of them looked abused or frightened. Quite the contrary. They were well coiffed, well spoken, jovial. What someone older and more experienced might have viewed with suspicion seemed like a wonderful opportunity to me, a naive twenty-two-year-old whose teen years were spent in a postage-stamp-size town. *For once I might fit*, I thought. I felt fortunate, like I had just been inducted into a sorority.

"Natalya has told me so much about you," Jeffrey said coolly. "It's great to finally meet you, Sarah." We chatted, with him confirming the details Natalya had shared. The cinema was massive, with floor after floor of escalators. On the way up, we continued talking about my family, my living situation in the city, my passion for design. He homed in on my background, though he questioned me more casually than Natalya had. Why did I want to go to FIT? What led me to drop out of Queen Margaret University? How did I become interested in design? What part of Cape Town did my father live in, and where in the UK was my mom? How many siblings did I have? Did I have any family or friends in the

United States? How long did I plan to stay? He hung on to my every word, and I basked in his close listening.

Inside the theater, I sat beside Jeffrey as Natalya had instructed. The other girls were on either side of us, in the same row. At one point during the film, Jeffrey gently and quite briefly patted my knee. There was nothing untoward or sinister about the exchange, no sexual vibe whatsoever. In fact, Jeffrey felt fatherly to me, unsurprisingly given my familial history. On the way out, he and I talked a bit more about my goal to apply to FIT as soon as possible. He politely thanked me, waved goodbye at the door, and that was that. *I wonder if he liked me*, I thought on the way home. I could only hope. Unbeknownst to me, I had just passed an admissions interview with flying colors.

A few days later, Natalya rang me. I was out of it, and honestly, borderline suicidal. Coke messes with the body's serotonin levels, and I was coming down hard from a binge. I was also spiraling into depression. The crisp winds of September had turned cold in October, and I didn't have a steady income. My savings were diminishing, between rent payments to Tom, taxi rides everywhere (I hadn't yet mastered the subway system), and going out for every meal or buying ready-to-eat packaged food at the pricey Upper East Side markets (I refused to cook in Tom's filthy kitchen). I had planned to apply to FIT for the spring semester and would need to support myself until then, as well as all the way through school. I had no solid plan for how I would do that. I just knew I couldn't stay with Tom indefinitely. That's the head space I was in when Natalya made an offer.

"Jeffrey's arranging a girls' trip to his island in the Caribbean," she said. "He's invited you to come along for four days. You wouldn't have to bring much . . . everything we need is there. I've been to his place many times. It's fun." She needed to know my answer right then, she said, because it was wheels up the next day. I hastily agreed, again reasoning that if Natalya had visited, it must be safe. And also, I was possibly *this close* to my FIT dream, and surrounded by a wonderful female support system that seemed to like me for me. As someone fresh off the boat from Scotland, I had absolutely no context for what seemed peculiar versus plausible in this Promised Land called America. *Maybe miracles happen here*. I certainly wasn't going to let a windfall slip away.

Natalya's reassurance put me at ease. "It'll be great," she repeated. "He really just wants to help you. He truly liked you at the movies." Surely, my friend, a girl around my age, wouldn't knowingly lead me into a horror flick. How I wish I'd been more discerning, emotionally whole and mature enough, to ask Natalya a series of probing questions, just as she had asked me at the club. *How, exactly, is this man assisting you? What must you do in exchange? When did you meet him, where in the city do you live, what did you and the other girls do when you last visited his island?* On and on.

What would set off a series of ding-ding-dings today just didn't for me then. My traumas, the pandemonium of my early years and the choices that flowed from that chaos, had long ago disabled my alarm system. I had no boundaries. I had no bells. I had no reason, I felt, to flee. As I saw it, I had two clear options. Behind door number one was the terror, the profound humiliation, of having to return to survival sex work. Behind door number two was what appeared to be the chance of a lifetime. I didn't know this man, but whatever he had to offer certainly had to be better than what I had escaped. I didn't consider that there might be a third door, or others. I just excitedly packed my bags and mentioned to no one, not even Tom, where I was going. As I gathered my things, I thought of my dad's beaming face when I would eventually tell him I had enrolled at FIT.

I didn't Google Jeffrey that autumn. I saw no need, given my immediate trust in Natalya and in women overall. Like many girls, I'd been raised with the notion that females are generally safe, and Stranger Dangers are almost always male. Also, my archaic flip phone had no Internet. If I had looked Jeffrey up, I would've discovered remarkably less than we now know about the depths of his depravity. The media hadn't yet trained its searchlight on him, or on sexual predators in general.

"Me Too" was then in its infancy. Tarana Burke coined the phrase in 2006, yet the movement gathered steam only a decade later when Ashley Judd accused Harvey Weinstein of assault. When I arrived in New York, Matt Lauer was still an anchor on NBC's *Today Show*; USA Gymnastics team doctor Larry Nassar was surreptitiously raping young female gymnasts; and Bill and Melinda French Gates were still married, with Bill having yet to describe his relationship with Jeffrey as a "huge mistake," which he declared in a 2021 CNN interview. Investigative journalist Ronan Farrow was still eons away from weaponizing his pen with reports on Les Moonves at CBS, former New York attorney general Eric Tradd Schneiderman, and, of course, Weinstein (and by the way, in July 2006—just a few months before my fated movie date—Harvey had his photo taken with Jeffrey and Ghislaine at Windsor Castle, at the eighteenth birthday party of Princess Beatrice, the eldest daughter of Prince Andrew and Fergie). When my life intersected with Jeffrey's, his reputation showed cracks in its foundation, but his world was nowhere near crumbling. A Google search, had I done one, would have confirmed what I believed, and what Natalya's presence reinforced: He was wealthy. He was generous. He was trustworthy.

The year before I met the man I thought would become my fairy godfather, a fourteen-year-old girl told police that she had been molested by him at his Palm Beach, Florida, mansion, the secluded home he had purchased in 1990. That's when the Palm Beach Police first widened its eyes. In the summer of 2006, weeks before I sat next to Jeffrey in a theater, the FBI opened its own investigation. And yet the media were slow to pick up their bullhorn on the most pervasive sex-trafficking story of our generation. Power and affluence, as they are prone to do, lent Jeffrey and his copilot Ghislaine a protective veneer. There were rumors then, even allegations, of Jeffrey's predation. And he was a master at squashing negative press, as he seemingly did with a 2003 *Vanity Fair* piece.

NPR got that scoop. In a 2019 episode, "A Dead Cat, a Lawyer's Call and a Five-Figure Donation: How Media Fell Short on Epstein," the outlet reported that Graydon Carter, then editor in chief of *Vanity Fair*, assigned a profile on Jeffrey to investigative journalist Vicky Ward. The intent was to shed light on this financier who flew Bill Clinton and other power brokers on his private jet. What was the source of his wealth? His only publicly known client was Leslie Wexner, the billionaire founder of L Brands (The Limited and Victoria's Secret). And why were these gorgeous gazelles, many of whom appeared underage, swarming around him? "I've known Jeff for fifteen years," Donald Trump told *New York* magazine in 2002. "Terrific guy. It is even said that he likes beautiful women as much as I do, and many of them are on the younger side." There had to be a story behind such accounts.

Vicky's detective work led her to Maria Farmer and her sister, Annie, the first survivors to report Jeffrey's and Ghislaine's alleged abuse to the FBI. Vicky planned to include the sisters' claims in her piece, but according to NPR, Jeffrey showed up at Graydon's office ahead of publication and urged him not to include reporting on his proclivity for adolescent-looking girls. John Connolly, then a contributing editor for *Vanity Fair*, as well as a crime reporter, says he witnessed the confrontation. "And he was torturing Graydon," he said, presumably with threats. Vicky's piece, "The Talented Mr. Epstein," did run—but without the sisters' accounts. (Graydon has said the story lacked the three sources required to meet the publication's "legal threshold" for publication; Maria, Annie, and their mother have stated that they each gave on-the-record interviews to Vicky.)

Enter the first of two troubling discoveries. John Connolly reports that, soon after Vicky's story ran, Graydon found a bullet outside his Manhattan door. "That wasn't a coincidence," John told NPR, though any link to Jeffrey is unproven. John, undeterred, continued talking with women in Jeffrey's orbit. Graydon next found the bloody, detached head of a cat in the front yard of his home in Connecticut. "It was done to intimidate," John said. "No question about it." Again, there's no evidence of Jeffrey's involvement. But it strains credulity that these incidents were purely random, at the exact time when Graydon and his team were possibly getting close to blowing the cover off Jeffrey's trafficking ring, or at least increasing scrutiny on his behavior. The NPR piece details other ways the media may have been intimidated into silence by Jeffrey and his attorneys.

When I met Jeffrey, he was viewed as a Gatsby-like figure and philanthropist who, though mysterious and eccentric, certainly hadn't been shunned. He moved freely in elite circles, unscathed and apparently unfazed by the rape allegations and resulting investigations. He knew he was in the FBI's crosshairs when we met, yet he had the hubris, or maybe the shameless narcissism, to continue targeting young women and training Natalya to recruit them. I believe that he lured me in, at age twenty-two, as a strategy to begin claiming that his rapes were consensual affairs. That first fourteen-year-old Palm Beach accuser was young enough to don a milk mustache. If he skewed older, he'd throw the press and FBI agents off his foul scent.

Courtney Wild confirms Jeffrey's preference for victims barely out of their tweens. Julie K. Brown, the investigative journalist whose *Miami Herald* series "Perversion of Justice" brought widespread attention to the Epstein case, interviewed Courtney in 2018. In "How a Future Trump Cabinet Member Gave a Serial Abuser the Deal of a Lifetime," Courtney—recruited by the pedophile in 2002 when she was fourteen and still in braces—says she eventually began delivering other girls to Jeffrey as a way to earn money. "By the time I was 16, I had probably brought him 70 to 80 girls who were all 14 and 15 years old," she says. Courtney told potential recruits they could earn two hundred to three hundred dollars in cash to give a wealthy man a massage. If, after a violation, a girl seemed too frightened to return, Jeffrey dangled a carrot: he would pay her to bring him fresh faces. "[Jeffrey] told me he wanted them as young as I could find them," Courtney says. She and others have said that if they brought Jeffrey a girl in her twenties, he flatly rejected her. His apparent appetite for the flat-chested and prepubescent was insatiable. "If I had a girl to bring him at breakfast, lunch, and dinner, then that's how many times I would go [to his home] a day," Courtney says. "He wanted as many girls as I could get him. It was never enough."

While Jeffrey was reeling in children by the dozens, Ghislaine was shoring up his social credibility. Her close ties with the billionaire reportedly began in the early nineties, an ocean away from the country she was reared in. Ghislaine Noelle Marion Maxwell is the youngest of nine, daughter of Robert Maxwell (born in Czechoslovakia as Ján Ludvík Hyman Binyamin Hoch in 1923), an up-from-poverty media magnate and war refugee who fought against the Nazis and lost his family in Auschwitz, and Elisabeth "Betty" Maxwell (née Meynard), a French-born, Sorbonne-educated scholar and renowned Holocaust researcher. The couple wed in 1945. They welcomed Ghislaine on Christmas Day in 1961.

Tragedy struck forty-eight hours later. Ghislaine's brother Michael, then fifteen and the family's first born, was in a car accident that left him in a coma. He died in 1967. Beneath that heaviness—similar to the sort permeating my mother's girlhood after her brother, Tommy, became crippled—Ghislaine grew up in Oxford at Headington Hill Hall, the storied estate where Oscar Wilde once took to the dance floor during a May Day ball in 1878. Decades later, under Robert's ownership, the fifty-plus-room property also housed the offices of Pergamon Press, his publishing company.

Ghislaine was the quintessential daddy's girl, the sort I've never been. Robert, stern with an explosive temper, had a soft spot for his youngest—however such sentimentality manifests in a man known as wrathful (in Elisabeth Maxwell's 1994 autobiography, *A Mind of My Own: My Life with Robert Maxwell*, she characterizes her husband as a tyrant who terrorized the family). Ghislaine came of age in the rarified air and company of nobility, the same universe my grandparents inhabited. The girl whose father nicknamed her "Sprat," as in a small fish, was educated in top prep schools, including Marlborough College, the Wiltshire boarding school attended by Kate Middleton, Her Royal Highness the Duchess of Cambridge. Ghislaine went on to attend Oxford's Balliol College, where she continued establishing herself as one of England's most glamorous socialites, and no doubt polished the four languages she reportedly speaks. Robert, who served as an MP for Buckingham between 1964 and 1970, hosted opulent gatherings with the haut monde, affairs Ghislaine attended. Royals and aristocrats were her dinner mates; she rubbed shoulders with Princess Diana (a photo exists of the two meeting in 1984, at a film premiere of *Indiana Jones and the Temple of Doom*). Journalist Anne McElvoy, Ghislaine's Oxford classmate, recalls their university days. "Ghislaine, while herself on a pedestal of privilege, was armed with a self-confidence so bulletproof that she could joke about 'making Diana (later Princess of Wales) cry' in a world where 'teasing' about everything from the wrong boyfriend to the wrong designer could come uncomfortably close to bullying," she wrote in the *Evening Standard* in 2020.

Robert doted on Ghislaine as he directed her career path. When he became owner of Oxford United Football Club, he tapped his then bushy-haired, twenty-two-year-old daughter as director in 1984. Later, when he bought the failing New York *Daily News*, in a bid to best his publishing rival Rupert Murdoch at News Corp, Ghislaine was among his most ardent supporters, a daughter and a friend. By then, her address book bulged with contacts such as Prince Andrew, who is accused of rape by one Epstein-Maxwell survivor, and of sexual misconduct by another. (He strongly denies both claims.) His name and those of other powerful leaders eventually filled Jeffrey's black book. Robert, who remained besotted with his youngest into her adulthood, bought a twenty-million-dollar, 180-foot super yacht in 1987. He named it *Lady Ghislaine*.

The press baron perished on that boat four years later. Beneath a cloud of mystery that lingers to this moment, Robert, a suspected fraudster and Mossad spy, was found floating, naked and arms splayed out, off the coast of the Canary Islands. That was on November 5, 1991, when Ghislaine was almost thirty. Some have

speculated Robert's death at age sixty-eight was suicidal or acci-
dental (Spanish investigators declared he'd had a heart attack and
fell overboard). Ghislaine has unequivocally stated she believes
that he was murdered. What surfaced, after his death, was indis-
putable evidence that he had robbed Peter to pay himself. He had
defaulted on millions in loans and attempted to cover the shortfall
by siphoning a reported $670 million that went missing from his
employees' pensions. The discovery tarnished the Maxwell name
and put a damper on Ghislaine's social life. The family's Oxford
estate was auctioned, as was its London flat. Questions over her
brothers' involvement in their father's pilfering turned the British
public and press against them. Kevin and Ian Maxwell, who had
worked alongside their dad and have denied knowledge of his
wrongdoing, were arrested on fraud charges. They were eventually acquitted. Their patriarch, buried on the Mount of Olives in
Jerusalem, left a legacy of scandal.

Ghislaine took her tears abroad. Perhaps looking for the kind
of reset that led me to Scotland, she moved to New York in 1991.
She took an Upper East Side apartment and became a business
consultant in name; in practice, she was a burgeoning socialite
in a new city that conferred on her the opportunity for reinven-
tion, just as it did for me. It's unclear when exactly she met Jeffrey
(it has been speculated that the financier may have aided Robert
Maxwell in hiding money in off-shore accounts, and that he and
Jeffrey became acquainted before Robert's death). What's apparent is Ghislaine's connection with Jeffrey in 1993. She knew him
well enough to arrange a raunchy musical toast as his fortieth
birthday surprise.

Christopher Mason has recounted the story in the docuseries *Epstein's Shadow: Ghislaine Maxwell*, as well as to *Vanity Fair*. In a July 2020 piece, "Ghislaine Maxwell's Haunting Fortieth Birthday Present to Jeffrey Epstein," the British journalist, then a friend of Ghislaine, says he was commissioned by the media heiress to pen a tasteless song. It seems she was dating Jeffrey, says Christopher, who had been in touch with Ghislaine in the months after her dad's passing. "The impression was that all the money was gone, and she had gone from privilege and private planes to penury and dejection," he told *Vanity Fair*. "She didn't have any specific ideas [about a career], but she was young and energetic and ambitious, and I felt fairly sure that, even though she was in a precarious state, she would somehow rise, phoenix-like. And sure enough, she did, within a year. . . . It appeared that she was suddenly flush again and dating Jeffrey."

Ghislaine dictated the content to be included in Jeffrey's birthday tribute. "She wanted me to mention that when Epstein was teaching at the Dalton School, he was the subject of many schoolgirl crushes," Christopher recalls. He thought such a mention was "kind of an odd thing to want in a song about a man who appears to be your boyfriend. But she clearly thought that that was something that was going to amuse him. Another odd thing that she wanted me to say was that he had 24-hour erections." At the black-tie affair, the serenade, delivered a cappella by Christopher, went over swimmingly with the seven or so men gathered—among them Les Wexner. The song was met with "laughter, amusement, applause. . . . It seemed to have lots of good references that they were all guffawing over," says Christopher. Jeffrey's lust for young girls seemed an open secret in his circle. Was Ghislaine truly then Jeffrey's girlfriend? Fuck buddy? Bestie? Madam who groomed his prey? I can attest only to the latter.

Whatever the nature of the pair's relationship, it proved mutually beneficial. In a years-long quid pro quo, Ghislaine lent Jeffrey Old World sophistication and entrée to an A-list social club including Prince Andrew, Elon Musk, and the Clintons—none of whom, just by association with Ghislaine and Jeffrey, are proved to have unclean hands. Jeffrey yearned for such access, as well as for a steady stream of victims to feed his sickness. Ghislaine needed a benefactor to replace her father, who left the family largely bankrupt. In that exchange, Jeffrey paid Ghislaine well enough for her to purchase, in 2000, the five-story, seven-thousand-square-foot residence she shared with Max, the Yorkshire terrier she named after her father. (Ghislaine's home at the time, located at 116 East Sixty-Fifth Street, was only a few blocks from the colossal mansion Jeffrey then owned. Her property was bought by an anonymous LLC, with an address matching the office of J. Epstein & Co.)

Investment banker Euan Rellie is a Brit who frequented Ghislaine's parties in her Upper East Side mansion—gatherings that, over the years, included royals and billionaires, as well as members of the Kennedy and Rockefeller dynasties, *The Times* of London reported in 2011. Euan was as confused as many about how, exactly, his friend and Jeffrey partnered. In a July 2019 *New York Times* piece, "Scrutiny for 'Lady of the House' Who Was Long Entangled with Jeffrey Epstein," Euan said Ghislaine "seemed to be half ex-girlfriend, half employee, half best friend, and fixer."

While Ghislaine denies any knowledge of the sex ring and has called her accusers liars, multiple survivors have continued to state that, whether the pair were bedmates or sidekicks, Ghislaine served as Jeffrey's lead groomer and procurer—identifying, targeting, and trapping the vulnerable in the way Natalya and Jeffrey did me. Ghislaine and Jeffrey's romance seemed long over the year I was cornered. But they were definitely still fellow demons in a lewd underworld.

When I met Jeffrey, I believe that he intended to come across as friendly and fatherly, as well as to listen closely. Violation begins with interviewing, before a victim's skirt is ever forced up. "Sexual grooming is the process of deliberately establishing a connection with an individual in order to prepare that person for sexual exploitation," writes psychologist Dr. Grant Sinnamon, founder of Bela Menso Brain and Behaviour Centre in Queensland, Australia. His research on the topic has been published in the book *The Psychology of Criminal and Antisocial Behavior*. He identifies seven stages of adult sexual grooming, a process parallel to that of grooming a child:

1. Selecting victims (the way Ghislaine did when she reportedly prowled Central Park in search of troubled girls).

2. Gathering information (That's why Natalya quizzed me. She verified I was sexually open, emotionally and financially desperate, and hoping to get into FIT.)

3. Gaining personal connection (building trust).

4. Meeting the need and establishing credentials.

5. Priming the target.

6. Instigating sexual contact.

7. Maintaining control of the victim by alternating constantly between sticks (abuse) and carrots (praise), as well as by making threats and offering bribes.

The first three stages happened in rapid succession for me. The latter steps, the apex of my horror, were just one frightening plane ride away.

7

Hell's Runway

On the morning of the four-hour flight, Natalya reiterated the rules: no cigarettes or booze. She also added a new one—no cameras allowed on the island. I didn't mind the restrictions, given what I dreamed of receiving in exchange. It would be a lovely retreat during which I could relax and recuperate while spending time with other girls in a wholesome environment. When it came to the smoking, however, my stallion nature kicked in. I sneaked a few ciggies into my bag, in case a craving overtook me.

A driver picked us up and took us to Teterboro, a private airport in New Jersey catering to wealthy jet owners. During the ride, Natalya casually mentioned, "Jeffrey sometimes likes for us to give him massages, and he might ask you to do that. It's no big deal, nothing sexual, just something he's into. All of us girls have massaged him before. It's cool." She mentioned that he would pay me a couple of hundred dollars in cash for the service, if he even requested it of me. None of this struck me as strange, particularly since she clearly stated there was nothing unseemly involved.

Back in Edinburgh, I'd enjoyed many relaxing massages, as a treat to myself in a spa. It made sense that Jeffrey, a billionaire philanthropist who I then presumed must have a demanding schedule, liked to unwind during his downtime. My hope was that he would be keen enough on me to crack open the door to FIT. I had absolutely no training or skill as a masseuse. But if he needed a basic back or foot rub, one he would even pay me for, that sounded like a gilded gateway to my education.

The airport officials glanced at our passports and waved us through to the tarmac. We were the first to board. I gazed around at the posh beige furnishings, as amazed to be on a private jet as I had been to gawk at Manhattan's skyscrapers. I noted a bed in the rear and figured that Jeffrey, a globetrotting businessman, must use it to get some shut-eye during his long-haul, overnight flights. Natalya and I took our seats. Soon after, several others came up the stairs: Jeffrey, in an oversized sweatshirt and jeans; Nadia Marcinkova, a petite blonde woman Natalya told me was Jeffrey's Slovakian girlfriend (*You see? He has a girlfriend. . . . I'm safe.*); and Sarah Kellen, Jeffrey's longtime lieutenant—the one he described to the *New York Times* as an extension of his brain. Jeffrey was the only man, other than the pilot. All the women appeared around my age, give or take a few years. And every single one of them was pretty enough, even if not statuesque enough, to model.

As we settled in, Natalya, with a grin and a girlish giggle, leaned toward me and said, "We're going to have such a good time this weekend! I cannot wait for you to see the island." I let out a slow breath and sat back in the cushioned leather seat, giddy that I, a girl tucked away near a Scotland forest a few years earlier, was now traveling like a celebrity. I mean, who gets to fly on a private jet—to a private *island*—so soon after coming to America? This was the lifestyle of the privileged. Kim Kardashian and Kylie Jenner have their own jets. So do Jay-Z and Beyoncé, Tom Cruise, and Taylor Swift. I had awakened that morning to the grunge of Tom's apartment. Now here I sat in aircraft bliss, experiencing what only the most affluent regularly could. My dad and stepmom would be impressed, and likely even a touch envious.

Nadia, decked out in designer gear, flopped down across from me and glared, her stare burning a hole through my forehead. I had no idea what prompted her iciness, but I ignored it. Jeffrey said hello and was as friendly as he had been at the theater. After takeoff, Natalya began massaging Jeffrey's hands, at his request. Nadia rubbed his shoulders. "Sarah," he asked me after a few moments, "would you mind please massaging my feet?" Natalya and I traded a knowing glance as Jeffrey, seated across from me, lifted his cashmere-socked foot. Natalya set aside his hands to give me a brief lesson. "This is how you do it," she coached, applying deep pressure to his foot. I did my best to mimic her, though my effort made Jeffrey recoil. Natalya repeated her demonstration. My second attempt was better, but not much. Still, I and the others kneaded our fingers into Jeffrey for a half hour or so. We then all helped ourselves to beverages and snacks and spaced out around the aircraft. Everyone nodded off.

Or at least they feigned deep sleep. I must have dozed off briefly myself, and I awakened to the unspeakable. Jeffrey and Nadia were having full-on intercourse on the bed near the back of the plane. She straddled Jeffrey, who was on his back. She humped vigorously. At one point, he flipped her over onto her side and began thrusting from her rear. Sweat dripped from his temples. Nadia's face was flush. And never once, while this freak show was unfolding, did anyone around me stir. My body tensed up into fight-or-flight mode, as adrenaline coursed through me. To be certain I wasn't having a nightmare, I closed my eyes, took a breath, and reopened my lids. It was all so terrifyingly real.

I swiveled around and tried to catch Natalya's eye, but her lids, like everyone's, were clasped shut. *What the hell is happening right now?* I thought. *And why are they all ignoring this?* I had seen some weird shit, courtesy of Rick, but never had I seen a couple have sex in public. No one moved. No one awakened from their faux sleep amid sounds so loud it was impossible not to have heard them. When Jeffrey and Nadia reached orgasm, their wails reverberating through the cabin, not a single eyelash fluttered.

I slid down in my seat and joined the others in fake snoozing, but, inside, I was wide awake and yelling at the top of my lungs. My brain raced with ideas of how I could get off this flight and return to the city. *Could I somehow alert the captain, awaken Natalya, claim to both that I'm so ill we need to land, pretend to be having chest pains?* The panic, the pace of my heart galloping, thrust me into paralysis. I stared at the exit door. When you're thirty-five thousand feet above the Atlantic, that door leads not to a tarmac but to an infinite expanse of blue, thousands of miles deep. I turned my head to the side, asked God to help me, and tried, but failed, to fall asleep in earnest. Moments later, I parted my lids ever so slightly when I heard movement. Jeffrey and Nadia had gotten dressed and were settling back into their seats, as if the porn show they had put on had never taken place.

By the time we landed two hours later, I had embraced a similar denial: I'd resigned myself to seeing the trip through. Was I frightened? Beyond the expressible. Yet I was more scared of what bailing might mean for me . . . the funeral of my FIT dream. My desire to finally become someone, to be made whole, felt all-consuming. I rationalized Jeffrey's public erotica as some fetish for exhibitionism. *To each his own*, I told myself. *That must be his thing.* An enduring impact of childhood sexual trauma, particularly if it remains secret, is that it conditions the survivor to stifle his or her own wails. It blurs all boundaries, makes the person question his or her instincts and visceral outrage. The survivor swallows the sorrow, shoves it into the farthest corner of the body. The rape and its hiding together muffle one's voice. That is what I experienced on that flight to hell: a silencing of my spirit. At least with Nadia in the picture, I reasoned, Jeffrey's peculiar sexual appetite would be satiated, and hence not affect me. *If I can just hang around in his life long enough to make him like me*, I thought, *I'll be that much closer to a college acceptance letter.*

When we landed in St. Thomas, the doorway to the US Virgin Islands, Jeffrey collected our passports and handed them to the airport officials. They didn't even look at them. When the blue books were given back to Jeffrey in a stack, he glanced around at us and said, "I'll hold on to these for safekeeping." Our bags were searched, and Jeffrey took my phone, reminding me of the no-camera policy . . . though I'm not even sure my dinosaur phone was capable of snapping photos. During his search, Jeffrey overlooked my cigarettes. Natalya, I could tell, was avoiding me altogether, averting her gaze each time I stared at her with "What the fuck?!" emblazoned on my brow. I couldn't wait to talk with her alone, to flood her with the questions drowning my insides.

St. Thomas appeared to be a stone's throw from the island. On a clear day, you can look across and see it a few miles away. We boarded a speedboat to Little St. James, a seventy-plus-acre paradise he called "Little St. Jeff's," surrounded by gleaming shades of cerulean. I pushed the plane ride to the back of my head, relished the sunlight on my face, glimpsed the lush greenery in the distance, glanced up at the clouds smiling over us. "Why don't you drive?" Jeffrey said, offering me the wheel. I clutched on and held it steady, felt like a Bond girl as the wind whipped through my bob. *What happens in the air stays in the air*, I told myself, gripping the helm tighter. I wouldn't let it steal my heaven on earth.

Warmth abounded on the dock. Jeffrey's staff members—the chef, a few groundskeepers, and an elderly couple, our caretakers, and Jeffrey's bodyguard and personal trainer, Igor Zinoviev—greeted us one by one. "Welcome!" they chirped, smiling as they helped us with our bags. Meeting Catherine and Miles Alexander, the sweet older couple, immediately lowered my blood pressure. They were a mom-and-pop type, charming and gracious, with South African accents that made me feel at home. Catherine showed me and the other girls to the bungalow, chatting and laughing as we walked. "If you need anything at all," she said once we reached the door, "please let me know." I nodded and entered the cavernous space. Nadia and Natalya came in with me. Sarah

Kellen and Jeffrey sauntered toward the main house, a short distance away.

The bungalow was lined with twin beds, a few on each wall. "This is my spot," Nadia said with annoyance in her tone. She placed her bag on the bed closest to the bathroom. I thought it odd that Jeffrey's girlfriend, his apparent sex toy, would stay with us rather than in his bedroom. I put my small bag on the twin farthest from Nadia's and looked over at Natalya, who was settling in on the bed next to mine. She refused to meet eyes. None of us spoke while we unpacked. I opened my chest of drawers, filled with lingerie I took out one piece at a time. The items were all from Victoria's Secret. None were skimpy or racy. Rather, there was an array of colorful slip dresses and swimsuits a preteen might wear. I sat down on the bed and ran my palm across the luxurious sheets, white and velvety soft. In our shared bathroom, the cabinets overflowed with expensive products such as Crème de la Mer. The staff had asked us to change into our beach gear ahead of dinner. I put on a bikini and a sundress over it.

At dusk, we gathered on the stone patio of the main house, a colossal estate overlooking the sea. The chef prepared our scrumptious meal, made on request, and we gathered around in chairs, with tray tables in front of us. On that first evening, Jeffrey sat next to me. "I need a massage," he announced when we had finished eating. *Another one?* I thought. Two girls shot up and began working on his back. He asked me to join in. As I rubbed his bare feet, smooth as my bald head at birth, he recoiled. "That's not how you do it!" he shouted. I froze. "Natalya, will you show her the right technique again?" She brushed me aside and began massaging, as he continued reprimanding me. "I want it *stronger*," he kept saying. "You're not doing it right." Gone was the Mister Rogers I had met in the cinema. In his place was a schmuck who was yelling orders at me.

My first evening on the island passed without incident, though amid continuing scowls from Natalya. She literally would not talk to me. That evening in the bungalow, under a top sheet with a thread count clearly in the high hundreds, I slid into another round of justification. I convinced myself that the terror in the sky and the tyranny on the patio were anomalies that would vanish. The next morning's lovely breakfast supported that view. We all gathered on the outside terrace as the chef served us mouthwatering breakfast burritos, and Catherine brought us tea. More massages on the patio followed, though this time Jeffrey raised less complaint about my amateur kneading. *Exhale.* I spent the day exploring the island, breathing in the stillness, gazing at the seabirds winging over the vast ocean. I was mostly on my own, which wasn't the retreat I had imagined, yet the quiet time was restorative. I returned to the bungalow just before nightfall, with Natalya still shunning me. Exhausted with her snubs, I marched up to her and said, "Can we talk?" She rolled her eyes and scampered off.

Later that evening, in the shadows, she addressed me for the first time. "Jeffrey wants to see you," she said robotically. I sat up from bed and stared at her. "*Now?*" I said. She nodded. "What the fuck is happening, Natalya?" I asked, searching her eyes. She was stone-faced. She led me down a dark path toward the estate, along a side of the property I hadn't yet seen. We entered the main house, and I peered around. Jeffrey wasn't there. She continued walking, guiding me toward Jeffrey's suite. She stopped, looked me up and down, and then knocked twice and left me there. Jeffrey, clad in a white bathrobe, creaked open the door. What happened next, in that abyss, churns inside me still.

In the years since I arrived at Little St. James, I've replayed every moment of that journey in my head, from the sedan ride to Teterboro and the spectacle to follow, to the smiles awaiting me at the port. Frame by frame, tear by tear, I recall the angst, the wondering, the question I still have: How could a queue of unwitting deer be led to their slaughter, while others, knowing their coming fate, stood by in total silence?

Take Jeffrey's pilot. I have the flight log for one of my trips onboard Jeffrey's "Lolita Express," and scrawled near the log's bottom is the pilot's signature: David Rodgers. The *Daily Mirror* interviewed David for a January 2021 piece, "Pilot 'Flew Prince Andrew' on Private Jet and 'Sex Slave Was on Board.'" David served as Jeffrey's captain between 1995 and 2013, a span of nearly two decades, operating various aircraft in Jeffrey's fleet (it included a pair of Gulfstreams, at least one helicopter, and a Boeing 727, the Lolita Express I first flew on). Journalist Christopher Bucktin tracked down the pilot in Florida. He asked him about his years in Jeffrey's employment, and whether he had flown survivor Virginia Giuffre—who has accused Prince Andrew of having sex with her at Jeffrey and Ghislaine's behest, a claim Prince Andrew emphatically denies. David said pithily, "I can't talk."

David's flight logs, however, whisper part of the tale. In July 2019, the *New York Times* reported that Manhattan prosecutors in the Epstein case issued subpoenas to David and another of Jeffrey's longtime pilots, Larry Visoski (according to a 2021 report in *Vanity Fair*, Larry is cooperating with the FBI). And both pilots have turned over flight logs to investigators. The *Daily Mirror* quotes a source close to David. "[He] has complied with the FBI and others investigating those who enabled Jeffrey's offending," the source says. "He was trusted with his most prized and high-profile friends, not only the prince, but Bill Clinton too. He is adamant he didn't see any wrongdoing as he flew Epstein, his cronies, and the girls around." Larry has said he knew that underage girls flew on Jeffrey's planes but saw no sexual activity between them.

Adamant. I'll take David at his word, yet I've often questioned whether he suspected inappropriate behavior. Only he can say for certain. Yes, he was in his cockpit, at the wheel, focused on flying the plane. But during his eighteen years in Jeffrey's service, did the father of two not once lift a brow at the steady flow of girls and young women climbing onboard the aircraft? And even if he could not overhear the kind of loud moaning that startled me on my maiden flight, did he have even an inkling that he might have been enabling a pedophile? Virginia Giuffre (née Roberts) has said in court records that she was recruited, at age seventeen, as Jeffrey and Ghislaine's "sex slave" for two years, during which time she says she was forced into intercourse with Prince Andrew on three occasions. The second son of Queen Elizabeth II not only says Virginia's accusations are outright fabrications; he claims he has no memory of ever meeting her, even though she has publicly released a photo showing him with his arm around her waist in the Belgravia, London, home of Ghislaine—who beams behind them in the picture. Virginia says Jeffrey took the photo. The Duke of York has attempted to cast doubt on the authenticity of the image by calling it a "photograph of a photograph of a photograph," yet he notably doesn't explain whether such purported duplicates are, in fact, based on an authentic original.

Back to the pilot. Virginia maintains that she flew to all of Jeffrey's properties, as well as overseas, with both him and Ghislaine—and David, flight logs indicate, was sometimes in the cockpit. In 2020, a federal judge unsealed court documents including Virginia's 2016 deposition in a civil case against Ghislaine. Virginia's claims therein are damning. She describes "constant orgies" with Ghislaine and Jeffrey on the island—and in the air. When a lawyer questioned her about where the sex acts with Ghislaine occurred, she said, "It happened all the time on the planes." That must have included atop the bed where I witnessed Nadia and Jeffrey's mile-high exhibition. Separately, Virginia has said that, while on Pedophile Island, Ghislaine and Jeffrey asked her to carry a baby for them—and then hand that child over for them to raise. (Virginia's attorney, Bradley Edwards, revealed this account in his book, *Relentless Pursuit: My Fight for the Victims of Jeffrey Epstein*.) For her surrogacy service, Virginia says she was offered a home and an allowance of two hundred thousand dollars a month. She insisted that they first help her become certified as a massage therapist. Months later, when they sent her to Thailand for her certification—as well as to bring back a new recruit—Virginia finally escaped her enslavers.

All of this happened right under the noses of the cheerful
South African couple, Catherine and Miles Alexander, who
worked for Jeffrey beginning in 1999 and moved on in 2007.
They shared their story with the *Daily Mail* in March 2011. They
say Jeffrey's July 2006 arrest warrant is what lifted the scales from
their eyes. Catherine, upon discovering the warrant on a desk
in Jeffrey's island home, rushed to tell her husband, "Something
bad is going on." Jeffrey, however, soon convinced them he was a
victim of entrapment. So they stayed a while longer, until Catherine insisted they quit. "I saw some girls who I thought were
very young-looking—about 16 or 17 easily—and it bugged me
because I have a daughter and, although she was in her 20s, I
didn't like the idea that another woman's child was in that situation. I didn't feel comfortable about it," she told the *Daily Mail*.
"They looked like they had stepped out of an underwear cata-
logue. They walked around with very few clothes on or lounged
around by the pool with nothing on. It was like that most of the
time. I was concerned about their ages. A few of them looked
very young and I couldn't help but wonder if their mothers knew
where they were. . . . One very young-looking girl was called
Tila. I just thought, *You really shouldn't be here*, but I made myself switch off as I had no proof." Added Miles: "I took the view
that what went on behind closed doors was not my business and
it is not my place to judge. If anything was going on we didn't
want to know. . . . Our job was about discretion. We have a clear
conscience that we didn't witness anything untoward. Whatever
went on at the other houses—and yes, we heard things from
other members of staff—it didn't, to my knowledge, happen at

our property." Catherine and Miles have not been charged with any wrongdoing.

The couple has since reportedly retired to my homeland, South Africa, and how I wish I could sit across from them today. I applaud them for finally moving on from Jeffrey, yet their long service prompts, for me, thoughts most disquieting. There's a faint, ever-thinning line between "discretion" and complicity. In Miles's own reported words, he did not *want* to know what was happening during his eight years of service—and one will never glimpse what one has deemed too grievous to behold. Denial clouds vision. On my first trip to Jeffrey's island and the many to follow, Catherine and Miles were in and out of our bungalow and all over the main house, bringing us tea, shepherding us around, ensuring our days flowed smoothly from dawn to sunset. Interesting to me that Miles reportedly claims he saw nothing that would have raised his suspicions of impropriety.

This couple—like the chefs who prepared our meals and the grounds people who cared for the property—were so intimately involved in the day-to-day operations of Orgy Island that I'm left to ponder whether Miles's stated choice for blindness absolves him of all responsibility, particularly since he's quoted as saying that he heard whisperings from the staff at Jeffrey's other properties. He and his wife may not have been in the room when a girl was being savagely raped, just as the pilots may not have seen pedophilia playing out in real time. Yet their very presence in Jeffrey's world, whether or not they knew of his assaults, normalized the environment. That attendance lent Jeffrey the same social credibility that Ghislaine's place at his side did. The moment that couple greeted me, I lowered my guard. I believe that was Jeffrey's calculated intent—disarmament of his prey.

I spoke to the *Miami Herald* for a September 2019 piece, "'When You Are In, You Can't Get Out': Women Describe How Jeffrey Epstein Controlled Them." What I said then I still fervently believe: everyone around us had to know Jeffrey and Ghislaine were attacking us because we looked so broken. The only way you could have missed the signs is if you had decided they did not exist. Bradley Edwards, the author of *Relentless Pursuit: My Fight for the Victims of Jeffrey Epstein*—and the Fort Lauderdale civil trial lawyer who has capably represented me and scores of other survivors—knows the nuances of what he calls "Epstein's Process," the psychology of how a degenerate operates. "[Jeffrey] would find out [his victims] have no home, no car, that they need a place to live, and he would provide a place to live," he told the *Miami Herald* in the same piece for which I commented. "He can get you to the best doctors. Sometimes he would do that and sometimes he wouldn't do that, but the promise was real because as soon as you walk into his house and see there are legitimate cooks, chefs, and assistants, everybody catering to him—it gives this air of legitimacy. I mean, everybody in this whole entire mansion can't possibly be running an illegal sex trafficking operation, right?" That's precisely what I thought when I first entered a hell attended by Jeffrey's full staff.

Sealed lips, Jeffrey knew, could be purchased. He invested heavily in his frequent port of entry, St. Thomas. A *New York Times* piece, "Epstein's Island, 'Little St. Jeff's': A Hideaway Where Money Bought Influence," sheds light on how Jeffrey operated.

Dorothy Ruth Coulter—
my grandmother, married to the
2nd Baron of Drumochter.

Grandpa—
the 2nd Baron of Drumochter.

Dad, kissing me as a baby.

Me as a little girl.

Kyllachy Estate in Tomatin, Scotland—my grandfather's house. He owned land for miles. It was used for fishing and hunting.

Mum and me.

Me as a little girl.

My second mum, Miriam. She was with me since I was a baby and left the family not long after this photo was taken. She had had enough of my mum. My heart broke in a million pieces.

The family before Dad and Mum got divorced.

I was a swimming champion in primary school
and frequently broke my own records.

This is me after I graduated from high school in Scotland and a few years before I left Edinburgh to start fresh in New York City. I met Jeffrey weeks later.

Me on Jeffrey Epstein's speedboat, going to the island.

Jean-Luc Brunel, island-hopping in Jeffrey's helicopter. This happened frequently, with many other guests coming to the island on their helicopters, so who came and went on Jeffrey's island was never recorded. This photo was taken during a New Year's trip in 2006/2007 on the island.

Me (*far left*), Jane Doe (*left*), Nadia (*right*), and Jane Doe (*far right*). The other victims and I had to pose for photos all the time, and we always had to smile or we'd get in trouble. I was emotionally dying inside and my fake smiling was starting to wear thin. Where these photos ended up being sent, and to whom, I will never know.

Jeffrey made it a rule never to photograph him . . . ever. We were not allowed any cameras or phones on the island. This is him on a quad bike riding around during a New Year's trip in 2006/2007 on his island.

Jean-Luc and Ghislaine, having fun on Jeffrey's island. They were the best of friends. New Year's trip, 2006/2007.

Jane Doe (*far left*); Sarah Kellen (*left*); me, looking distressed; Jane Doe (*far right*). They were all eating large meals and I was allowed to eat only what Jeffrey gave me. This was on Jeffrey's island. New Year's trip, 2006/2007.

Ghislaine on her phone, again at the outside dining table on the island, New Year's 2006/2007. This happened all day long. She was always on her multiple phones. I often overheard her organizing when the next girls were to arrive either at the island or at the New York mansion upon Jeffrey's return to New York.

Nadia, pretending to stab Jane Doe with a knife. Nadia, Jeffrey, and Ghislaine thought it was funny. The other victims and I were terrified. New Year's trip, 2006/2007, on the island.

Jean-Luc and me on the beach on the island. Jean-Luc was repeatedly taking photos of us and asked us to model and look sexy for him. I always felt very uncomfortable. New Year's trip, 2006/2007.

Jean-Luc asked me to pose for him on the island. New Year's trip 2006/2007.

Peter Mandleson and Jeffrey. Peter worked under UK prime ministers Tony Blair and Gordon Brown. Peter was the European commissioner for trade for the UK under Prime Minister Tony Blair when this photo was taken. This was on one of the islands near Jeffrey's island. Jean-Luc is taking the photo. New Year's trip, 2006/2007. Peter has not been charged with any wrongdoing.

Sarah Kellen on the island. She was on her laptop or had it beside her. I witnessed her organizing existing and new victims for Jeffrey. Rotation, rotation, rotation.

Me with Ghislaine's dog, Max, in the girls' bungalow on Jeffrey's island. This was on one of my many trips where Ghislaine was present. Either 2006 or 2007.

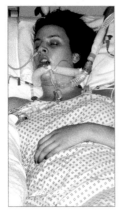

Jeffrey's plea bargain ("sweetheart deal") had catastrophic effects on me, and I tried to commit suicide. I was in a coma for a month, had thirty-seven brain seizures, got pneumonia, and contracted MRSA. My family was told that I wouldn't make it, and they all flew in to say goodbye to me. August 16, 2008.

Me in Mas de Bondia, looking at an apartment when we went into hiding.

Before I came forward. I was so happy and loving life!

Our day in court, when the survivors addressed Judge Berman. August 29, 2019, New York.

Outside Jeffrey's house in Paris, October 2019, waiting to confront his staff members about why they never came forward.

"He cultivated close ties to the islands' political and financial elite," journalist Steve Eder writes. "He employed a governor's wife. He hired an architecture firm owned by that governor's uncle. He donated money, sponsored scholarships and even gave dozens of computers to a local lawmaker to distribute." Jeffrey bought Little St. James in 1998 for the nosebleed price of $7.95 million. As he settled in, he showed his neighboring island financial goodwill, which may have much to do with how easily he breezed in and out of the St. Thomas port, with planes overflowing with victims. Money talks—and it can also elicit a chilling hush.

At least one of Jeffrey's staff members confronted him, reports *Newsweek* in a September 2020 piece, "Jeffrey Epstein Told Housekeeper Victims 'Only Want Money' After Warning." Juan Alessi, who worked as a house manager in Jeffrey's Florida mansion, says he didn't know his boss was raping girls and women—though in 2005, he told Palm Beach police that he cleaned Jeffrey's vibrators after his massages, according to the *Newsweek* piece. Still, at one point Juan spoke up. On the podcast *Broken: Seeking Justice*, Juan says he told Jeffrey, "One of these girls one day is going to get you in trouble." Juan, who notes Jeffrey often mispronounced his name as "John," said Jeffrey told him, "John, they only want money." Virginia Giuffre was part of that podcast conversation. Juan told her, "I feel so sorry that this jerk was in the end abusing little girls. It's sickening. He could have had all the women in the world."

Juan, even if rather feebly, did raise his voice. Scores of others never will. That may be in part due to what scientists call the bystander effect—the tendency for those witnessing inhumanity to acquiesce, specifically when others are present at the crime scene. Social psychologists Bibb Latané and John Darley pioneered research on the theory in the 1960s, after a twenty-eight-year-old woman, Kitty Genovese, was attacked near her Kew Gardens, Queens, apartment. The assailant approached her late one evening as she was returning from her shift at a bar. When she tried to flee, he caught up to her and then stabbed her in the back with a hunting knife. Multiple neighbors awakened as the woman begged for her life. Some, thinking it might have been a domestic brawl, turned away. The point is that those who saw or overhead the attack did not intervene—instead leaving it to others to step in, or at a minimum, to call the police.

Latané and Darley's research, though challenged by some, underscores a phenomenon perhaps applicable to the Epstein-Maxwell machine: the greater the number of people who are present at an atrocity, the less likely those onlookers are to act. There will always be valiant bystanders, society's whistleblowers. But if a crime happens in front of a crowd, most there are inclined to feel, *Let someone else handle it*. Elie Wiesel, the political activist, scholar, and Holocaust survivor who withstood untold barbarism, left humanity with a love note on the subject. "Let us remember: what hurts the victim most is not the cruelty of the oppressor but the silence of the bystander." Dr. Martin Luther King Jr., another great with a front-row seat to brutality, put it his own way. "In the end, we will remember not the words of our enemies, but the silence of our friends."

Power—who has it and who lacks it, which is tied inextricably to our socially conditioned view of that—has everything to do with who will be muted and whose misdeeds will be ignored. In the 2021 book *Credible: Why We Doubt Accusers and Protect Abusers*, Dr. Deborah Tuerkheimer writes on the dynamics at play in the Maxwell-Epstein case. "Epstein's exploitation of teenage girls was defended by a culture—and a legal system—disposed to preserve his interests. Undue regard for abusers found many outlets: the employees who helped Epstein capitalize on the desperation of marginalized girls and women; the influential friends who knew or should have known of his ongoing predations; the media that looked the other way rather than expose his crimes; the Florida prosecutors who bestowed the sweetheart deal kept secret from his victims; the jailers who allowed him to leave the grounds daily, during which time he allegedly abused at least one young woman; the New York prosecutors who recommended a downward departure from sex offender classification guidelines; the power brokers who by association legitimized his conduct. This treatment reveals 'the broad cultural antipathy toward treating sexual abuse as real harm,' as [writer Moira] Donegan explains. It also shows that teenage girls matter much less than powerful men."

I'm curious about not only what quiets bystanders but also what lends predators such brazenness. Jeffrey and Ghislaine did little to hide their widespread operation. Ghislaine was bold enough to reportedly roam parks and malls in search of fresh meat, as well as to allegedly take part in sexual acts with minors who could and did report her to authorities. Jeffrey held up his proverbial middle finger at all of us, even after the Palm Beach Police Department and the FBI began investigating him. I cannot get inside a pedophile's head, but I can speculate on his and Ghislaine's motivations. By the time I met them, society had long since taught them the chief tenet of elitism: you are invincible, armored against all censure. In their world of Entitlement with a capital E, the rules applying to the hoi polloi, the unclean masses, are mere suggestions for the ruling class—the masters of the universe they believe themselves to be. Jeffrey and Ghislaine felt that they were above the law, above the underlings whose lives they eviscerated. It was with this understating that they operated so conspicuously. They must have realized that their crimes had spilled into public view. Their status bestowed on them the luxury of not having to care. They didn't think they would ever be held fully accountable for their actions. Over and over that had been proved to them, years before I stepped into Jeffrey's suite.

8

Trapped

Jeffrey's bedroom was cold for a hellhole. It had to be eighty degrees under the stars, balmy enough for me to walk from the bungalow in a slip dress and an orange bikini. Yet when I entered his suite, my nipples hardened at the freezing blast of air. I glanced around. In one corner sat a massive bed, fitted seemingly with the same brand of white sheets that were on our twins. A massage table stood in the room's center. He locked the door and stared at me, eyes devoid of soul.

"You've been massaging me," he said in a gravelly voice. "And now it's my turn to be your masseuse." As he inched closer, I recoiled, looked over at the doorknob. "Take off your dress, Sarah," he said. I did as he ordered and slid onto the table, face up and trembling. He slathered oil on my body one slow stroke at a time, first on my thighs. Next on my stomach. And last, after pulling down my bikini bottom with his icy fingers, right onto my vulva. "Tonight I'm going to teach you how to be a woman," he said. He gazed at me and did not blink. I began weeping, soft cries, the whimpers of a child. He took off his robe and exposed his erect body, sallow and clammy, despite the chill. He then picked up a vibrating massager, one larger than I'd even seen, and turned it on. At the sound of the loud buzzing I tried to sit up, but he pushed down hard on my chest.

With one hand he began masturbating, occasionally stopping to lick his palm for lubrication. With his other hand, he pressed the massager onto my clitoris as I half-sobbed, half-screamed, "Stop . . . please stop!" He didn't flinch, as all forms of "no means no" fell on his deaf ears. "Just breathe," he leaned toward me and whispered, as if my nurturer, not torturer. "You're hurting me!" I shrieked. "Now be a good girl and climax," he said as he turned up the vibrator. "If you can come for me, I'll let you go." My body, drained of its fight, went limp at the futility. There was no way out. The pressure of the massager eventually triggered an orgasm, a purely physiological reaction. I lay there, lifeless, breathless, cheeks covered in snot and tears, as he continued jerking off. His semen, an angry white blob, exploded across my midsection. His face, his neck, his eyes were all crimson as he let out the sound of death. He put on his robe, mechanically, and unlocked the door. I scurried from the table, pulled on my dress, ran wailing from the suite, my insides still quaking from the vibrator. Every person on the island had to have heard my screams, but they went unacknowledged, ignored, swallowed whole by the surrounding darkness. And there, in the hall as I was storming out, stood another girl, summoned to her slaughter.

I cried my way back to the bungalow and collapsed, chest heaving, onto my bed. The room was dark. Natalya wasn't there. The others, who had to have heard my sniveling, did not stir. Moments later, the door creaked open. Natalya tiptoed in and toward my bed. She sat on the edge and ran her warm palm across my back. I wept into my pillow. "Sarah, this is what you have to do," she said quietly, mother-like. "I'm sorry, but this is the deal." I looked up from my pillow and reached to embrace her, but she stood and backed away. "I can't" was all she said. Her deer had been trapped. Her assignment, the pretense, was over. Her payment, I would learn, had been rendered.

A sadist, per *Merriam-Webster's*, is "a person who takes pleasure in inflicting pain, punishment, or humiliation on others." I glimpsed such gratification in Jeffrey's eyes, spotted it on his brow. The louder I howled, a guttural weeping, the harder he pushed on my clit. He grinned in delight at my anguish, took joy in trapping his prey. Dr. Grant Sinnamon, the psychologist who outlined adult grooming's seven stages, has identified two personality types most likely to be rapists. Jeffrey showed characteristics of both.

The first is the narcissistic predator. "This predator is likely to have either a high, but fragile, or a low self-esteem," writes Sinnamon in *The Psychology of Criminal and Antisocial Behavior*. "The narcissistic belief that they are better than others, and therefore that their needs and desires are ultimately more deserving of fulfillment, are not necessarily supported by their low or high-fragile self-esteem, and this incongruence fuels their motivation and behavior. Fantasies about power, success, and their own attractiveness and value to others blur reality, and exaggerations about personal achievement, success, and talent may be made." Such assailants, Sinnamon notes, may also be driven by retaliatory rage—a feeling that they have been robbed of due recognition by society, by a certain community, by an individual. More generally, however, this rapist's attacks are an extension of an inflated ego, one he or she props up by dominating the weak. Jeffrey, I believe, raped females because it fueled his sense of self-importance. Others have called him enigmatic, a man of great mystery. I call him a megalomaniac.

The antisocial predator is the second sort, overlapping with the previous. Both exploit while in pursuit of power. Yet this rapist most often does so through subterfuge. "The antisocial personality type will thrive on the elements of the grooming process that involve pretense and deception," observes Sinnamon. "These actions provide the antisocial predator with a sense of domination of others and an opportunity for them to exercise their devious superiority, and to exhibit their contempt for others and to show the manner in which all others are no more than playthings to be toyed with at the predator's discretion." In short, this predator lies his or her way to dominance—as Jeffrey did throughout my grooming process. Each type seeks to wrest control.

The *New York Times*, in October 2017, explores rapists' common characteristics. In "What Experts Know About Men Who Rape," journalist Heather Murphy parses the intricacies. She notes: "These men begin early, studies find. They may associate with others who also commit sexual violence. They usually deny that they have raped women even as they admit to nonconsensual sex. Clarifying these and other patterns, many researchers say, is the most realistic path toward curtailing behaviors that cause so much pain." Volumes abound on the psychology of victims, fewer on the nature of attackers. Understanding the latter is the key to addressing sexual violence in our world. For every survivor whose claims we discredit, for all our smirking and victim blaming, our fixation on how low cut a woman's blouse was, we are shifting our focus off predators who will continue raping. While we're putting victims on trial, assailants are roaming free. As Heather reports, rapists begin early—and seldom, I suspect, do many violate just once. Jeffrey and Ghislaine's alleged corruption, which took place on multiple continents, may number in the high hundreds. We'll never know.

Dr. Neil Malamuth, the psychologist cited in Heather's piece, has studied sexual aggression for decades. In the article, he notes a trend among repeat offenders: they share similar stories of having been spurned during high school, hinting that "jocks and the football players got all the attractive women." I have no idea what experiences Jeffrey's sadism was rooted in, nor do I know how far back his violations go. When one reads between the lines of reports on his early years, few, if any conclusions can be drawn. Still, let us have a look.

The *Daily Beast*, in an August 2019 article, "Epstein's Coney Island Days: From Math Nerd to 'Arrogant Prick,'" surveys Jeffrey's background. The CliffsNotes version: Jeffrey, born in July 1953, grew up on New York's Coney Island in a working-class family. He's the eldest of two (his younger brother is Mark), reared by Seymour and Pauline Epstein, both children of immigrants. His father was a groundskeeper for the New York City Department of Parks, and his mother, a school aide. Neighbors recall Jeffrey as quiet, a talented pianist, and a math nerd whose natural brilliance with numbers awed even his parents. A neighbor of Jeffrey's, mentioned in the *Daily Beast* profile, once posted on Facebook, "He was just an average boy, very smart in math, slightly overweight, freckles, always smiling. There was absolutely no indication at that time of the vile, disturbed man that he was to become." Perhaps not, but I do wonder whether the "slightly overweight" description had anything to do with who Jeffrey turned out to be. A Google search yields a photo of a shirtless, wild-haired Jeffrey in 1969, an image that deepens that query for me. Did the so-called nerd ever yearn for the attention of female classmates, like the adolescent girls he had become so fixated on raping? Was Jeffrey overlooked by such girls during his own teen years? It's impossible to know for sure, yet easy to see how a clue may lurk in that neighborhood.

His math brilliance carried him fast and far. By age sixteen, having skipped two grades, he was already enrolled at Cooper Union in Manhattan's East Village, taking high-level math courses. By eighteen, he was studying mathematical physiology at New York University but didn't graduate. At twenty-one, in 1974, his knack for numbers offset his dropout status. He landed a job as a math and physics teacher at Dalton, the Upper East Side prep school. The *New York Times* once noted Jeffrey's flamboyance during his Dalton days. He at times donned a fur coat, open shirt revealing his chest and a gold chain, and reportedly had a reputation for ogling his female students. In a July 2019 profile on Jeffrey, the *Times* quotes Scott Spizer, a 1976 graduate of Dalton, who took notice of Jeffrey's lingering, inappropriate attention to girls in the halls and classrooms. "I can remember thinking at the time, 'This is wrong,'" Scott said. Jeffrey was never officially accused of any improprieties at the school, though one girl, who spoke to the *Times* anonymously, was disturbed by his attempt to spend time with her away from school; another student recalls he attended an off-campus party meant for students. Jeffrey's brief tenure ended in dismissal. An interim headmaster in those years, Peter Branch, says, "Epstein was a young teacher who didn't come up to snuff. So, ultimately, he was asked to leave." A contact of Jeffrey's at Dalton, along with Jeffrey's numbers intelligence, paved his way to Wall Street soon after.

Other reporting adds pencil strokes to Jeffrey's emerging silhouette. According to a July 2019 *Miami Herald* profile of the financier, Alan Greenberg, CEO at Bear Stearns, was so impressed with Jeffrey—a fellow so-called PSD, as in poor, smart, and desperate to be rich—that he hired him in 1976, when Jeffrey was twenty-three. He rose rapidly through the ranks, from assistant to office trader to limited partner by 1980, just four years after joining the investment bank. He was a millionaire before age thirty. He was also reportedly a gifted schmoozer who connected well with the firm's most wealthy clients, using his mastery of the US tax code, for instance, to help the rich lower their tax bills. Jeffrey, however, left Stearns in 1981, after a possible "Reg D" violation—he reportedly lent money to a friend to buy stock, claiming he didn't realize the transgression. In "The Talented Mr. Epstein"—that *Vanity Fair* story that ran without the Farmer sisters' accounts—Vicky Ward reports that he started his own money management firm, J. Epstein & Co. Then, sometime between 1986 and 1989, he met his one known billionaire client, Les Wexner of Victoria's Secret—as in the brand of lingerie filling my bungalow drawer when I arrived on Pedophile Island.

When, during that journey, did the math whiz morph into a serial rapist? I know only that he did. He showed little, if any, remorse for his actions, even gloated over his crimes. He once bragged to the *New York Post*, "I'm not a sexual predator, I'm an 'offender.' . . . It's the difference between a murderer and a person who steals a bagel." He said this following the 2008 sweetheart deal he received, thanks to what I see as the failure of Alex Acosta and others. If they had done their duties, he would have been thrown in prison for life. On the topic of Jeffrey's hubris, journalist Megan Garber has reported on it in a July 2019 *Atlantic* piece, "When Jeffrey Epstein Joked About Sex Abuse." Wrote Megan: "Epstein's private jet was widely known as the 'Lolita Express.' (Bill Clinton traveled on the plane; so did, reportedly, Prince Andrew, and Kevin Spacey, and Donald Trump.) When the writer Vicky Ward profiled Epstein for a 2003 article in *Vanity Fair*, she visited him in his Manhattan townhouse to conduct an interview. 'The only book he'd left out for me to see,' Ward would later write, 'was a paperback by the Marquis de Sade.' . . . In the guest bathrooms of his Palm Beach mansion, Epstein reportedly kept soaps molded to resemble genitalia." This was not a man intent on covering up his raping.

Survivor Johanna Sjoberg has testified to such arrogance. In a 2016 deposition, she said Jeffrey boasted to a friend of hers that he had taken a girl's virginity. Recalls Johanna: "He said, 'You see that girl over there laying by the pool?' She was 19. And he said, 'I just took her virginity.' And my friend Rachel was mortified." Johanna testified that she was recruited by Ghislaine to give Jeffrey "massages"—which she discovered, as I did, was code for rape. Ghislaine urged her to "finish the job" while massaging Jeffrey, by bringing him to orgasm. If she failed in that attempt, she was punished. Johanna, by the way, is one of two women accusing Prince Andrew of sexual impropriety—a claim that he, similarly to Jeffrey and Ghislaine's modus operandi, vehemently denies.

The evidence of Jeffrey's sickness, his rampant deceit and predation in adulthood, was obvious for anyone looking. Some signs, yes, were more visible than others. In 2019, after Jeffrey's arrest, authorities busted down the door of his New York City mansion. They found what they called a "vast trove of lewd photographs," many of them featuring young girls. The same was true during their raid of Orgy Island. Also discovered at his Fifth Avenue home: a locked safe containing a fake Saudi Arabian passport from the 1980s, along with cash and diamonds. These are, perhaps, clues in the conundrum of what creates a sexual predator—what transforms a wunderkind from a nice Brooklyn family into a mendacious, unrelenting madman.

There is a belief, erroneous as it is harmful, that an adult cannot be groomed and trafficked. If asked outright in a public setting whether someone "of age" can be violated in these ways, many would nod yes. *Absolutely. Of course. More power to #MeToo.* But later, in quiet dinner conversations with friends, and perhaps in unlit corners of the heart, there is dubiousness. Eyebrow raising. As well as the question I am often confronted with: How could you be trafficked and held against your will at age twenty-two? Childhood rape we understand and abhor. We cringe and clutch our pearls when we hear that a vulnerable fourteen-year-old in braces, like survivor Courtney Wild, has had her innocence wrenched away. Our hearts bleed for that baby, and they should. Yet there's less compassion, or understanding, for how a young adult could be trapped by Jeffrey and Ghislaine. "She should have known better," some say. "It's her fault. She got what she deserved. And where was her family, anyway? She was just a hooker looking for money." Such shaming is one reason many adult victims are loath to speak up. They often internalize that blame and shame, pointing the finger at themselves.

The paucity of research on adult sexual grooming itself is a form of dismissal. "The vast majority of the literature on grooming is focused on child sexual abuse and exploitation," acknowledges Dr. Grant Sinnamon. "However, personal and environmental grooming can and frequently does occur in the course of sexual exploitation and abuse of adults. Adult sexual grooming is analogous to child sexual grooming, and can be defined as any situation in which an adult is primed to permit themselves to be abused and/or exploited for sexual gratification of another."

A large power gap between rapist and victim sets the stage for adult exploitation. It's most easy for a predator to attack when such a differential exists—supervisor to employee, pastor to parishioner, politician to staffer, Harvey Weinstein to eighty-plus females, Jeffrey and Ghislaine to me. When a victim is desperate for money, says Sinnamon—or when there is, say, a major age difference between rapist and prey, or threats to one's safety or that of one's family—maintaining control becomes a cinch for a sociopath. "Having financial challenges can create immense pressure on individuals," he writes. "The predator is able to exploit this vulnerability by fulfilling a financial need such as paying an overdue account or other financial obligations. Money and financial security has been established in society as a panacea, and we therefore tend to place significant weight on those who obtain it or who are willing to assist us to obtain it. Predators are able to use this to gain trust and credibility very quickly with their victims."

That is exactly what happened to me and other survivors. Taken together, these factors—financial despair, fear for one's life or physical safety—create what psychologists call "coercive control." Regardless of a victim's age, cunning predators like Jeffrey and Ghislaine could and did establish that control. And Rick, my boyfriend in Edinburgh, raped me in the context of a romance, if our abusive connection can be called that. Is it even possible to have a so-called consensual relationship, sexual or otherwise, when a major power gap and brute force are involved? I don't think so. I also don't think one's age has anything to do with whether that abuse can happen. I am proof that it can. My life itself, from childhood on, had done most of Jeffrey and Ghislaine's grooming for them.

When I first began sharing my story in press interviews, message boards filled with vile comments afterward. I was called a prostitute—a description, as I've mentioned, I deplore, and have replaced with "survival sex worker." But to the point of the accusation, I have to ask: Would exchanging my body for groceries and rent strip me of my *human* rights? Because when someone says, "Oh, she's just a harlot who wants money"—the same notion Jeffrey reportedly once used to discredit his victims in the eyes of his confrontational house manager, Juan Alessi—the commenter is saying, in fact, that those languishing near the bottom of society's caste system are. Not. Even. Human. And while such unconscionable beliefs continue swirling through the culture, the Jeffreys and Ghislaines keep plowing and destroying.

Let's say a woman is an escort. She and the man she arrives to service in a hotel room have not signed any contract. Let's say she shows up and then decides, "This man is scaring me. I don't want to have sex with him." It is that woman's right, I firmly believe, to walk away *at any point*—to have her "no" be heard and respected, even though she is a survival sex worker. If that woman tries to flee and the man forces himself on her, he, with that coercion, becomes a rapist. Does that woman bear any responsibility for her choice—and I use the word while aware that survival sex workers have usually exhausted all or most of their real options—to be in that hotel room in the first place? She does. I own that I once put myself in such a vulnerable situation. Still, I am not a brute to be terrorized and discarded. I am a full, if wounded, human being. I have worth by nature of my existence alone. So does every person alive.

The dismissal of my humanity nearly cost me my voice, my right to put words to my horror. The wave of rebuke I received when I came forward initially led me to retreat and cower. It also made me question whether to ever tell The Story, to share what happened to me at the hands of Jeffrey and Ghislaine. That public skewering, that backlash most heartrending, became the reason I knew I must.

On the night that Jeffrey first raped me, I prayed it would be the last. From then on, I was sexually abused every single day, two or three times, as well as whenever I was on Orgy Island. It happened in the morning, right after breakfast. At midday, when my privates were still raw and bloodied from the violation just hours before. It took place during all hours of the evening, when I was often awakened in the bungalow and forced to go service Jeffrey. In a wicked game of cat and mouse he'd often say to me, "It's okay, Sarah, I won't rape you this time. Just come in my suite and run me a bath." I'd reluctantly slip into his bathroom and turn on the water, quietly exhaling that I had been spared. Moments later, he would enter naked, get in the tub and then pull me in, fully clothed, and have his way with me.

On my final day of that first weekend, Jeffrey upped his carrot-dangling game—as in stage seven of Sinnamon's model. "I know you don't have your own place in the city," he told me. "I've got a building on East Sixty-Sixth Street, not too far from my town-house. I can put you up in a beautiful apartment there." He promised he'd cover my other living expenses, even pay me some cash each week. He also offered to help me get a visa. Given the erotica I had witnessed, I imagined exiting his plane once it landed in New Jersey and bolting down the tarmac toward freedom. My stash of money, inching ever downward, made me nod yes even as my spirit screamed hell no. I didn't have a place of my own, and I needed one quite soon. Tom was nice, but the few hundred dollars he was charging me by the week meant I couldn't save up for a deposit on an apartment. Jeffrey's offer intersected with my financial distress.

Why did I remain connected with Jeffrey, even after I had discovered the sadist he was? I've asked myself that question many times, and I always come back to the same two answers. First, my desire to get into FIT, to finally brighten my father's countenance with the pride of my accomplishment, compelled me to endure assault. In years past, I had done exactly that to buy bread and butter. And now, as I saw it, college was the ultimate feast, a prize that seemed worth suffering for. My other reason, the one standing tallest, was, in a word, *fear*—the quaking in my chest, a profound anxiety that I might end up living on the streets. I had faced near homelessness in Edinburgh, in the weeks after I left college. My mother and I had almost lost her place in Petersfield, and she'd lived on the streets twice before then. I felt panicked that, without Jeffrey's cash and housing, I might slip back into long-term survival sex work, a life I was determined to leave in my rearview mirror. Being raped, in the short term, seemed better to me than living destitute in a foreign country.

Terror has a strong vibration, one haunting and continuous. I've felt the stomach churning, the racing of my heart that comes with the lack of necessities: a hot meal, water, rent, utilities, sanitary products. Unless you've been in that situation, or close to it, it is difficult to understand the fear, the shame, the breathlessness of that state. From the warmth of your living room, beneath a wool throw, you can forget winter's harshness, the bite of its howling winds. When you can comfortably or even uncomfortably make your house payment, if you've always had a roof over your head, you may have empathy for the homeless, yet you cannot truly know how it feels to teeter on the cliff edge of displacement. Words alone fail in conveying the trepidation.

I was also terrified of Jeffrey himself, by his threats to harm my loved ones and me. "If you ever tell anyone what happened here," he warned me on that first weekend, "I will kill you and your family." I believed him. *This is temporary*, I told myself. *I'll just be in his building long enough to get into school and put away some money for a studio.* My choice to stay, baffling as it may seem, was simply a desperation to live.

9

Ghislaine's Inferno

Ghislaine and her siblings gathered in London for a reunion on June 10, 2019—what would have been their father's ninety-sixth birthday, had he not been found, bloated and adrift, in the Atlantic. It was the first time in nearly a decade that the Maxwell children had been together. In a photo from that day, published with a 2021 story in *The Times* (London), Ghislaine sits front and center, smiling, with no awareness that her world will soon crumble. Four weeks later, her co-conspirator and once-upon-a-time boyfriend, Jeffrey, was arrested and charged with trafficking underage girls. One year later, almost to the day, the FBI broke through the locked gate of Ghislaine's New Hampshire hideaway and took her into custody. Her siblings tried to get her released on bail over the next several months. When that didn't work, her brother Ian motored up his spin machine. He told *The Times*, "The Ghislaine that we know has been buried in this caricature, this monstrous creature that has been invented as an abuser and a pimp."

The Ghislaine that Ian knew also kept secrets—major ones—from her brothers and sisters. By Ian's own admission to *The Times*, Ghislaine didn't tell her siblings that she had been married *for three years* when she saw them at that reunion. In fact, Ian and the others didn't even know Ghislaine was in a relationship with tech CEO Scott Borgerson, whom she had wed in 2016. Ian also says he met Jeffrey just once in person, way back in 1996. So while I understand Ian's impulse for tribe loyalty, and while I'm sure Ghislaine, like all of us, has various disparate faces, Ian is not qualified to say whether his baby sis behaved as a monster, an abuser, and a pimp while she partnered with Jeffrey for decades. He was not there. I spent many months in and out of Ghislaine's inferno, otherwise known as Pedophile Island. I experienced her savagery firsthand.

I've chosen the word *inferno*—a raging fire that chokes and destroys its victims—intentionally. That is the blazing abyss Ghislaine oversaw as she allegedly ran the most notorious sex-trafficking ring of our times. She hunted for troubled girls and women. She groomed them. She gathered other survivors and me on an island patio, to await our daily incineration. And in between, she kept her ear pressed to her BlackBerry as she captured more of the wounded, managed Jeffrey's affairs, and hobnobbed with the hundreds of prominent contacts in her Rolodex. If you believe the survivors who say she sexually violated them—and I do—Ghislaine is also an alleged rapist. She now claims that she knew nothing about the pyramid scheme she managed, if not engineered, as Jeffrey's commander of operations. Like Ian's attempt to rebrand her, that's rich.

I feared Ghislaine even before I met her. During my second trip to the island, Nadia, Sarah, and Jeffrey each made clear her role in the chain of command. "She's powerful, wealthy, and knows everyone," said Nadia, Jeffrey's supposed girlfriend. "Don't cross her." Sarah Kellen, Jeffrey's lieutenant, put it more mildly, but no less seriously. "Just stay out of her way and you'll be fine," she said, adding that I should regard her as royalty, just as I had my grandpa. Then, ahead of Ghislaine's arrival by helicopter, Jeffrey came out on the patio and sat near me. "A close friend of mine, Ghislaine, will be here shortly," he said. "She's in charge. Do whatever she tells you." *Powerhouse. Aristocrat. President. Got it.*

Five of us walked to the copter landing, on a part of the island I hadn't yet seen. At Jeffrey's direction, we queued up according to the food chain: Jeffrey, Sarah, and Nadia; the South African house caretaker, Miles; and the newbie, me. Moments later, the chopper descended and out strode Ghislaine with her Yorkshire terrier, Max. She certainly wasn't dressed like nobility or a glamorous millionaire. In fact, she looked frumpy, in a wrinkled sweatshirt and leggings, with short spiky black hair, scattered by the copter's blades. She made her way down the Airstair and greeted Jeffrey with an embrace, warm but not lingering. She nodded and smiled at the others before glancing over at me. "Hello, Ghislaine!" I chirped. She frowned, looked me up and down, and dismissed me with a glare that said "human rubbish." The inferno headmaster had arrived. So had my undoing.

After my first trip to Orgy Island a couple of weeks earlier, I moved into Jeffrey's apartment building, a high-rise located at 301

East Sixty-Sixth Street near Second Avenue. Many of the units, I would learn, were owned by Jeffrey's brother, real estate developer Mark Epstein of Ossa Properties (Mark denies any knowledge that Jeffrey used the building as a hub for his sex-trafficking operation). The building was a mile from what was then Jeffrey's twenty-eight-thousand-square-foot, forty-room mansion overlooking Central Park at 9 East Seventy-First Street. Hades II, it seems, had plenty of room for guests. The property was originally purchased by Jeffrey's one known billionaire client, Les Wexner.

Tom, the guy I had been staying with, was away on a work trip when I returned. As I awaited my move into Jeffrey's tower, I lived at Tom's place for another week. I left my last rent payment and his house key on a table, and then called to thank him. Crusty tub aside, he had been very good to me. Sarah Kellen—who is now living her happily ever after with NASCAR-driver husband Brian Vickers in a ten-million-dollar condo in SoHo, as she clarifies that she was also Jeffrey's rape victim—sent a car for me. Sarah and executive assistant Lesley Groff, Jeffrey's other second brain, would make such arrangements for me all the time—flights, car rides, phone calls, all of it. Multiple survivors have also claimed that they did such coordinating for Jeffrey and Ghislaine's recruits. I don't doubt that Sarah was sexually violated. But the assaults she endured seemingly gave her little pause in arranging Auschwitz for others, because what happened in Ghislaine's inferno gassed me to an emotional death.

Some of the fourteen- and fifteen-year-old babies recruited in Palm Beach told detectives that Sarah made their appointments; arranged their transportation to Jeffrey's mansion; set up their massage tables and lined up oils; and actually led them to their destruction. The *Daily Beast* reports that Sarah once maintained an interior design business, SLK Designs, at the 301 East Sixty-Sixth Street address where Jeffrey housed me. She also earned at least two hundred thousand dollars annually, like her colleague, Lesley, who says she didn't know females were being trafficked. Her perks and generous pay, and Sarah's—we're talking about over *years*, spanning a time when Lesley, a mother now in her fifties, worked for the pedophile—came bathed in the blood of children and young women.

My new apartment was a large one-bedroom on a high floor, with an amazing city view. With the exception of the cloud-blue walls, it looked like a standard midrange hotel room: couch and dining set, kitchenette, chest of drawers, and queen bed fitted with white cotton sheets. I unpacked my few belongings, sprawled out on the bed, and gazed up at the ceiling, feeling grateful to have housing, scared of what it would ultimately cost me. Jeffrey had handed me one hundred dollars before I left the island, enough to buy some basics—I would need to prepare my own food while in the city, as well as buy toiletries and such. That cash offering marked the start of a pattern. He would give me just enough money to get by for a few weeks and leave me pleading for more—that's stage seven, maintaining control, in Dr. Grant Sinnamon's grooming process. He kept me hungry so he could keep me imprisoned.

Isolation was key to Jeffrey's operation. I saw many pretty young women walk in and out of that building. I couldn't be sure which, if any, had been trafficked by Ghislaine and Jeffrey, though

I had my suspicions based on his apparent type: tall, pimple-sized breasts, emaciated, white—and often with those sorrowful eyes that whispered of deep brokenness. On the island, we would sometimes recognize one another: *Aren't you the girl who lives on my hall? Yes.* Still, we remained in our own little worlds, scared to converse even when Jeffrey and Ghislaine were not present. The fact that he kept us away from one another, and in rotation at the island and mansion, meant that we couldn't easily form attachments. If he and Ghislaine noticed I was getting along well with a particular girl, I'd often never see her again. He also stoked animosity between us, lavishing one victim with attention and shopping trips, only to shift the spotlight onto another favorite a few weeks later. (That's why I believe Nadia was not granted full entrée to Jeffrey's life and suite; he liked dangling the carrot of a "promotion" to the top rungs of his pyramid by ensuring none of his recruits ever felt secure in their status. It's also why I believe she was so nasty to me during my first plane ride to the island. Any new recruit was a potential threat to her place in her captor's world.) Jeffrey relished that we jockeyed for position. The more submissive a girl—and eager to move up the organizational chain—the more he rewarded her with gifts and a tender tone. It was another way he maintained dominance.

Jeffrey's townhouse, which was a private school before Les Wexner spent millions renovating it, was nouveau riche on steroids—as in a life-size female doll hanging from a chandelier. What I recall most clearly were walls lined with photos of the influential and the infamous, including Bill Clinton; Mohammed bin Salman, now the crown prince of Saudi Arabia; and Woody

Allen. *Vanity Fair* has reported that Jeffrey kept on an upper floor a large oil portrait of Bill Clinton dressed in a blue dress and heels. Other oddities reported: a stuffed tiger, giraffe, and black poodle, and rows of framed eyeballs, per reporter Vicky Ward; a gargantuan sculpture of a naked African; a chessboard with suggestively dressed figurines representing Jeffrey's staff, per the *New York Times*; and after his brief stint, more like a holiday, in a Florida county jail, a mural of a prison scene in which Jeffrey stands betwixt barbed wire and guards—a reminder, he said, that he could return to confinement.

Once when I arrived at Jeffrey's mansion, an attendant welcomed me at the door. In an upstairs bedroom, under the watchful eye of cameras we now know Jeffrey had installed, the sadist of course raped me, as well as made me perform oral sex on him. Other survivors have testified that he forced them to use strap-ons to penetrate one another; girl-on-girl orgies with a revolving cast of male power brokers seemed to be a theme in Jeffrey's world. If you find these details graphic, imagine living them. Ghislaine reportedly arranged numerous such orgies. And several survivors say she took part in their brutality.

One accuser, Jane Doe, a twenty-six-year-old Florida real estate broker, has said she was sexually assaulted by Ghislaine and Jeffrey at his Palm Beach mansion in 2008. After the attack, she testifies the two drove her to pick up her eight-year-old son and stopped the car "at a large body of water that was infested with alligators." States the filing: "Epstein then ushered the Plaintiff to the body of water and told her in explicit detail that, as had happened to other girls in the past, she would end up in this body of water and be devoured by the alligators, should she ever reveal what Epstein had done to her." Separately, in a civil case, Ghislaine has been charged with perjuring herself by denying she knew about the presence of underage girls at Jeffrey's properties. "She compounded her crimes by repeatedly lying in 2016, when she was questioned under oath," said Audrey Strauss, acting US attorney for the Southern District of New York, as reported in *The Wall Street Journal.* "Maxwell lied because the truth, as alleged, was almost unspeakable." Pardon me, brother Ian, but you have no bloody idea just how heinous and unutterable your sister's alleged crimes are.

I had been in hell for only a short time before its cadence of activity was established: Fly to the Caribbean, often by Lolita Express, but also via commercial flights booked by Sarah and Lesley. Endure violence daily. Return to apartment. Stay on call as Jeffrey's Fifth Avenue sex worker. Await next trip to Ghislaine's island inferno. Breathe, repeat, die.

Pedophile Island was a universe unto itself, with its own hierarchy, laws, rhythms, and even access points. Seafaring passersby couldn't just show up unannounced. If they had, they would have been met with a bed of angry sea urchins Jeffrey had placed all along the main shore. (Bradley Edwards, the attorney who has devoted much of his career to bringing Jeffrey and Ghislaine to justice, tried to come ashore in 2020. He wanted to explore the island as part of his research on the case. The urchins had other plans.) Out beyond the stingers, Jeffrey had an inflatable trampoline. I would have to ask to take a jetty out to it; when he granted me that privilege, he directed me to launch from a boat pier so I could avoid the urchins, at least the ones in the water.

No one had to tell me Ghislaine and Jeffrey weren't lovers by the time I entered the picture. Their energy was that of platonic familiarity, like siblings or best friends and definitely equals. She settled into the main house, though I don't know which room. I never saw her or her belongings in Jeffrey's suite, his rape cave, where he invited a revolving door of various girls. I also have no idea where those in the upper echelons of the pyramid—Sarah Kellen, Lesley Groff, Jean-Luc Brunel, and another of his accused recruiters, Jennifer Kalin—slept. I and the other girls were allowed in the bungalow. By the pool. In the kitchen. And we spent most of our time on the main-house patio overlooking the sea, on chairs and couches we were instructed to remain in. We did everything there: ate on tray tables; massaged Jeffrey at his whim; endured Ghislaine's interrogations; and, above all, waited to be goaded into Jeffrey's suite. Jean-Luc Brunel, the gregarious French scout who founded the MC2 modeling agency—and who is charged with providing Jeffrey with a pipeline of models-turned-hostages for at least a decade—was often on the patio with us. Ghislaine was the ringleader of the inferno, the enforcer. Sarah was her loyal VP. Lesley and Sarah stood as equals at that level. I probably made ten or so trips to the island over the months, and many others to the NYC mansion. The pecking order never shifted during my tenure in hell.

After my, shall we say, *memorable* first meeting with Ghislaine at the chopper, our connection spiraled south. I have a gift with animals, especially dogs, and her Yorkshire terrier, Max, went wild for me. He leapt up to greet me when I entered a room and also followed me around far more than he did his owner. Ghislaine detested me for it. "Come here, Max," she would coo when she noticed him near me. She'd spend the next hours either ignoring me or barking insults and orders. That was Cutthroat Ghislaine. At any moment, Sweet Ghislaine could make a sudden cameo. She'd be cozying up to me on the patio, all charming and chipper, with a grin that told me an invasion was imminent. Her questions were as endless as they were prying: What neighborhoods in Jo'burg were you reared in? What schools did you attend? Where do your mum and brother live now? What do your dad and step-mum do for a living and what are their contact details? Why do you want to go to FIT? On and on she went, digging for information she could use to cement her control. If I resisted answering, she momentarily turned empathetic. "It's okay, love . . . we can talk about it later."

Nonsense. When my rebellion continued beyond a few minutes, the nasty Ghislaine, ever lurking, pounced. She railed. She called me "filthy" and "repulsive." She even threatened to harm my parents if I didn't give her their phone numbers. I finally relented because I was deeply afraid that she and Jeffrey would send a sniper to South Africa. That is not an overstatement. It's why I tear up when strangers, many of whom are well meaning yet ignorant of the terror wafting through that world, ask me now, "Why didn't you just *leave*?" Because the fear, palpable and unflagging, truly paralyzed me. On one side of me sat a woman who allegedly threatened to feed a young mother to an alligator.

On the other side sat a sociopath who once raped me right in the foyer of his opulent New York townhouse. So, yes: I was petrified. And at age twenty-two and in a foreign country for the first time, I was every bit as scared as a fourteen-year-old would have been.

Amid the terror, my massage technique never improved. Ghislaine frequently shooed me aside so she could demonstrate how to best knead Jeffrey's back and feet. "This is how you do it, you prick," she would mutter as she strongly pressed her fingers into his pasty flesh. I can see why Ian and others are confused about who Ghislaine really is. She blew hot and cold, vacillating seamlessly between madam boss lady and nurturing mother figure. Which face she displayed depended on who was in the room or on the phone—the human rubbish she regarded me as, or the high-society guests she and Jeffrey hosted. Near the patio, I would hear her on her cell, in her most posh accent, saying, "Will the countess be available on next Friday evening for dinner? Please do let me know. I'd be delighted to have her join us." She and Jeffrey constantly dropped names—threats, really—to remind us of their reach, their access, their ability to either make or destroy our lives with a simple phone call. Those who attended Ghislaine's gatherings—celebrities, aristocrats, her fellow socialites—got Gracious Ghislaine. We got the conniving tyrant.

The First Commandment of Ghislaine's inferno, and really the only rule: remain ready to satisfy the sexual appetites of Jeffrey, who indeed seemed to have 24/7 erections. I don't know when, if ever, that man worked. There was a girl in his suite at nearly every hour. "Sarah, Jeffrey's waiting for you," Ghislaine would come out onto the patio and announce. "It's your turn." Initially, I resigned myself to the rapes, marched to the kill house and got my slaughtering done for the day, disconnected from my body as I once did with when Mum's inebriated lover found his way into my bed, dreamed of Scotland forests and underwater kingdoms, whispered pleas to God as Jeffrey sodomized me. My anus once bled so badly afterward I could not sit for two days. As my privates turned raw, I would refuse to go to the suite when Ghislaine summoned. "Get in there *now!*" she'd yell out onto the patio amid hours spent on her BlackBerry. When even Sarah couldn't force me off the couch, Ghislaine would step in again to remind me that my FIT dream hung in the balance . . . and homelessness was imminent. That usually got me moving.

Sarah, Natalya, Jennifer, and Ghislaine all urged me to Jeffrey's door for "massages"—a term they had to have understood meant rape. A half hour later, I would exit the suite weeping and limp my way to the bungalow to shower off Jeffrey's pungent semen. If all I was doing was rubbing his backside, why would I leave his room wailing? Why would I at times hide when they ordered me back to that room? Ghislaine not only had to have realized what was happening: she demanded that I and others participate. She didn't sexually assault me, as some have said she did them. Yet that woman attacked me daily with her presence, her premeditated grooming, her bullying, her utter disregard for my humanity.

A few weeks after I met Jeffrey, he and Ghislaine decided I was obese. That's when the body shaming began. "If you didn't eat for an entire month," Ghislaine once told me, "you'd still be overweight and disgusting." Relative to the two ballerinas I was there with a few times—Trina, five foot ten and about 115 pounds, and another girl, Mia, who was an inch or so shorter than Trina and maybe 5 pounds less . . . both were badly in need of a burger—I can see why they thought I was a pig. I simply wasn't skinny, not at five foot nine and 146 pounds. Before I landed in hell, I had been happy with my figure and confident in my body. On my first two island trips, I enjoyed the same meals everyone did: omelets and those breakfast burritos I loved; fresh fish or chicken and vegetables; various snacks the chefs organized in neatly stacked containers in the refrigerator.

That all changed after Ghislaine blew in. "Oh my God, you are an enormous heifer," she announced on the terrace one morning. She made me stand so she could point out the supposed flab on my frame. Sarah, Jennifer, Nadia, and the others snickered. Incidentally, Ghislaine, while slender, wasn't catwalk material. Perhaps that's one reason she became Jeffrey's spurned lover rather than his prized wife (*Vanity Fair* once reported she walked around wearing a large diamond ring Epstein once gave her, and that she was dying to marry the financier; he apparently felt differently). She and Jeffrey knew I wasn't fat. Yet they wanted to make me believe I was so that they could withhold my dream. "Jeffrey likes his girls slim," Ghislaine said. "Before we can get you into FIT, you'll need to get down to 114 pounds"—more than thirty pounds less than I then weighed. On my third trip to the island, Ghislaine forced me onto their made-up version of the Atkins Diet—stage one only. She instructed the chef to feed me cucumbers and tomatoes and a minute piece of meat—an amount one might feed a small child. There I would sit, surrounded by mouthwatering chicken piccata, as I nibbled at my slices. I drank a lot of water to try and make myself feel full. I would be so hungry some evenings that I'd lay awake, tummy protesting, as the skeletons around me slept.

Among Jeffrey's rotating recruits, I spent more time with Trina, the taller of the two dancers, than anyone. (Many of Jeffrey's victims were dancers or models, often from foreign countries. They fit his target demographic: young with an impoverished upbringing, one often including assault; underpaid in industries known for a rocky path to solvency; far away from loved ones; and, of course, tiny.) Trina was Jeffrey's next recruit after me. We met on my third trip, I think, and overlapped there four or five times. I could see how scared she was by her deer-in-the-headlights expression, the same one I wore upon arrival. In snatches of conversations on the patio, she shared her story. She was from eastern Europe. She had grown up in such extreme poverty in New York City that her parents had sold jewelry on the streets, just to earn enough money for bread. They were often homeless. Jeffrey promised to pay her way through ballet school, just as he had for Trina. After her first trip to Jeffrey's suite late one evening, she came back sobbing and doubled over onto her twin. I crept from my bed and rubbed her back, whispered, "It's okay, darling," as I wept with her. Because I was older—she had literally just turned eighteen—I wanted to spare her. A couple of times when Ghislaine called her to Jeffrey's suite, I volunteered in her place. Through quivering lips in the dark bungalow, she mouthed the words *thank you.*

The gratitude was short-lived. Because of how Jeffrey pitted us against one another—and also how tempting it was to ascend in his pyramid—Trina, a sweetheart with a subservient nature, began endearing herself to her abuser. Psychologists call that a trauma bond, or Stockholm Syndrome—a way to cope in lieu of escaping. "I'm Jeffrey's favorite" she'd brag while practicing her ballet moves in the bungalow. She had arrived as an innocent; captivity, however, slowly turned her into a mean-spirited queen bee, one sneering down on other girls to lock in her spot with Jeffrey. Once, when he flew us via copter to a nearby island—I can't recall which one—he purchased several designer pieces for Trina. I, the stallion, got nothing on that trip. He loved her subservience. He deplored my stiff back. I was never his or anyone's golden child, though he did buy me a couple of designer items over the months—the "carrot" phase of his constant grooming. Shortly after that, Trina disappeared from my view. I was sure she was dead. I would learn otherwise years later. In came the next round of meat in Jeffrey's shuffle. The faces changed, but the horrors never did. I saw my recruiter, Natalya, only once or twice more after she reeled me in. She was on to new victims, scouring more nightclubs, I'm sure. She did pop up, via text, after I had had a major row with Jeffrey over the way he and Ghislaine were starving me. "Jeffrey, he's just like that . . . don't worry about it," Natalya wrote. "Do as he says and all will be fine"— straight from the mouth of Jean-Luc, and from Ghislaine and Jeffrey's playbook. Their approach: if a victim turns mutinous, send in her recruiter to shove her back in line.

Jean-Luc was the seemingly good cop in an inferno overrun with harsh ones. After I would emerge from Jeffrey's suite in tears, he'd occasionally take me out on the quad bikes so I could catch my breath. Or he'd say, "If you want to succeed in life, you need to do what Jeffrey and Ghislaine tell you. They want you to lose weight, so lose weight. Follow their orders and everything will be fine." Jean-Luc, though he never sexually assaulted me, is seemingly as much of a sadist as his co-conspirators. In a 1998 exposé on *60 Minutes*, models accused him of drugging them; one said he raped her (Jean-Luc has denied the women's claims.). On days when Jeffrey berated me over my weight or threatened to obliterate my FIT dreams, Jean-Luc would come sidling up as a Samaritan, supposedly offering a salve but, ultimately, deepening my wound. Ghislaine did the same, playing Mother Teresa anytime Jeffrey went full-on Hitler, even comforting me following some rapes. "You'll be fine, dear," she would say while patting my shoulder. When she and Jean-Luc weren't laughing out on the patio, he was snapping pictures of us around the island. He'd yell, "Now pose!" Mia and Trina truly sexed it up for the camera, their raised cheekbones and pouty lips belying emotional decimation. I, by contrast, stood awkwardly as he snapped. I knew how to pose about as well as I knew how to rub Jeffrey's bunions.

Ghislaine's inferno was monitored around the clock. I stumbled on that awareness during my second time on the island. Though I didn't smoke on the first trip, I did later sneak in more ciggies. I had gone through coke withdrawal and was living on cucumbers. I needed my fags, thank you very much. One morning after Jeffrey raped me, I was desperate for a smoke, a release. I crept into a shower stall, one situated just outside our bungalow. I lit up and inhaled a few glorious puffs, closed my eyes and savored the nicotine rush. Moments later, Jeffrey raced through the bungalow, grabbed hold of my shoulders, and shook me as he shouted, "What are you doing *smoking*!?" I later spotted a microscopic camera just above the stall. Every inch of that island was under surveillance: bathrooms, bedrooms, kitchen, bungalow, shorelines. Jeffrey once called me into his private office in the main house and made me sit on his lap while he forced his fingers inside me. The whole time, he showed me film clips of the many people—leaders, friends, guests, family members—he had videotaped. He bragged that he'd never be caught or go to prison for his crimes. "I have tapes of every person who has ever been on my properties," he told me. He and Ghislaine used the existence of those tapes as leverage, to ensure their dirty laundry forever stayed in its hamper.

"How's my piglet today?" Ghislaine wandered out on the patio and asked me one morning, sometime in December 2006. I didn't even acknowledge her insult; by then, I had grown so used to the verbal battering that I'd almost become desensitized to it. I just slid down on the sofa as Sarah and Nadia giggled. "Come on," she said, "we need to go and photograph you." In silence I stood and followed her.

Cataloging my weight loss—that is what Ghislaine and Jeffrey dubbed the process of taking photographs of me every week to keep "on file." Unless I dropped to 114 pounds, I was reminded, FIT was off the table and the streets were my next postal code. These shoots occurred near the pool, an area visible from the patio we frequented. I can't recall whether I walked over to the bungalow to get a towel. I know only that, by the time I took my place on the pool deck in front of Ghislaine, I was completely naked beneath my bath sheet.

"Drop the towel," Ghislaine ordered as she prepared her camera. "Let's see how massive you are today." I slowly lowered the white terry cloth and set it to the side. I drew in a breath and glanced up over my shoulder. Sarah, Nadia, Mia, and Jennifer stood along the patio wall, staring down their judgments on my exposed flesh. "Move closer," Ghislaine shouted as she began snapping. "And *pose*, for God's sake. Can't you do anything right?" I clumsily threw back my shoulders and pasted on a smile as the sun, overpowering in its heat, unsparing in its brightness, joined in humiliating me. "I think you've gotten *fatter*," Ghislaine said as she clicked. Later, when Jeffrey saw the photos, he exploded. My life, my spirit, my self-regard had long ago gone up in flames. "Now get out of here," she barked. "It looks like we'll need to cut down on your cucumbers."

I had been violated in the cold of Jeffrey's suite, in the bedroom of his mansion, in the dark of his office. What happened on that deck, through Ghislaine's lens, is among the most degrading experiences of my life. Jeffrey raped my trembling body, over and over for months. Ghislaine, in a lone act just as wrenching, altered the shape of my soul.

10

Complicit

Cucumbers and weight gain seldom go hand in hand. A gourd of the green, even with its peel on, adds up to just thirty calories. That's why Ghislaine thought it odd that, after weeks of my cucumber-and tomato medleys alongside barely there protein, not only had I not lost weight, but I'd put *on* two pounds. What preceded my uptick and that body-shaming photo shoot explains why.

The issue began a few weeks after I was trafficked. I had been shuffling back and forth between my two islands of torture—Manhattan and Ghislaine's Caribbean inferno—and the rapes took an increasingly greater psychological toll. I slid into severe depression. My inner wild stallion lashed out in anger: at myself, at the world, and, most of all, at my captors. Jeffrey and I rowed constantly. Once when Ghislaine reprimanded me over my weight, I stormed out and cursed her. I threatened to take my life. After a series of detonations, Jeffrey interceded. "I'm going to call someone who can help you figure this out," he said, as if the source of my unraveling were a mystery. "I know a great psychiatrist, a friend of mine who can see you. And don't worry, I'll pay for everything."

Soon after I sat across from a brown-haired doctor, someplace in Midtown Manhattan. How I wish I could recall her name because I would love to have a word with her. "What brings you in today?" she asked, legs crossed as she clutched a clipboard, ready to take down notes. My truth came pouring forth. Through sobs, I told her about the trafficking, the rapes, Jeffrey's and Ghislaine's cruelty, all of it. I gave raw details, more graphic than those I've shared in these pages. She stared at me and nodded occasionally, but didn't speak until the end of our hourlong session. "Well, you're definitely depressed," she told me. *What a eureka, Einstein.* She also claimed that I was bipolar with ADHD. She said, "I'm going to write you three prescriptions . . . for Xanax, lithium, and Ritalin." She didn't test me or ask about my medical history. She didn't appear stunned, or even flinch, at my revelation that her friend Jeffrey was torturing me. She did not, in fact, look at me as she scribbled a trio of potent drugs with side effects I had no clue about. She just handed me a piece of paper and sent me back to hell.

I had no insurance. So when I reported the doctor's prescriptions to Jeffrey, he handed me cash to cover the cost. Within days of my first dose, I became a veritable Dracula. I wasn't just numb. I was catatonic, stumbling across streets into oncoming traffic, nearly falling over into the pond near the Central Park boathouse, slurring my words and sleeping for hours past daybreak. And almost immediately, courtesy of the lithium—a drug proved to cause significant weight gain in 25 percent of those who take it—I grew bloated. Meanwhile, Jeffrey and Ghislaine, who knew I was on lithium, watched in amusement as I piled on pounds. I believe that Jeffrey requested that his "friend," his apparent accomplice, write me that prescription. If I couldn't lose the pounds he had demanded I take off, he would never have to fulfill his promise to send me to FIT. He didn't intend to get me into school, I realize now. His and Ghislaine's sole goal was to wrest full control of me—to create a chemical dependence alongside my financial one. That's how you create a sex slave. That is how, in Sinnamon's seven stages of adult grooming, a predator maintains dominance over his or her victim. "There were doctors and psychiatrists and gynecologist visits," Virginia Giuffre told the *Miami Herald*. "There were dentists who whitened our teeth. There was a doctor who gave me Xanax. What doctor in their right mind, who is supposed to protect their patients, gives girls and young women Xanax?" One, apparently, who is in cahoots with Jeffrey Epstein.

That mindfuck set others in motion. If you've ever been on an antidepressant, then you know that skipping doses, even a few, can wreak havoc on your mood. I fought more with Jeffrey, not less, as I pleaded with him to consistently dole out the cash for my drugs. If I told him I was down to my last tablet, he would wait a few days before giving me cash—just enough to cover a month's supply, and not one pill more. The violent rapes continued. At least I was so comatose that one rape blurred into the next. I couldn't feel. I couldn't think. I couldn't speak my horror. All I could manage was a groan.

And a thank you. Because by then, I had formed a trauma bond of my own, a sense of indebtedness to Ghislaine for helping me craft my FIT entrance essay. I hadn't yet lost the weight. "But we can still begin on the essay," she told me, "so that it's ready after you drop the pounds." *Crafty.* In addition to her office in Jeffrey's mansion, Ghislaine had her own space in Midtown, I think . . . as a city newcomer, I hadn't yet mastered the neighborhood layout. Back from the island, I visited her in that office so we could review my drafts, as well as have general check-ins. She gave me pointers and even compliments, alternating between praise and criticism. "You're still much too fat," she would say in one breath, boasting about how she was able to stay slim with roller blading. (She once reportedly—and disgracefully, in my view—joked to a friend about how she kept herself so thin to appease Jeffrey. "I do it the way Nazis did it with the Jews, the Auschwitz diet," she said, according to a 2019 *Vanity Fair* piece. This alleged tastelessness from the daughter of a man who lost most of his family in Germany's concentration camps, and whose mother was a Holocaust researcher.) After hurling a stick at me, Ghislaine was soon on to a carrot. "You're a decent writer," she would say. "Well done, you." It breaks my heart now, from a place of greater wholeness, that I was grateful for her scraps of approval. I had unwittingly turned my warden into a mother figure.

My real mom and I talked occasionally during this period. She was still caught up in her own struggle, in her brave attempts at sobriety and peace. She expressed concern for me, could hear the sadness in my tone. I assured her all was fine, that I was on the doorstep of FIT and just needed to stay focused on my goal. She lit up at that news, as did my father and stepmom. I didn't want to involve any of them in the trap I had stumbled into, and I felt most protective of my dear brother. He was on his own, eking out a life in Jo'burg, barely able to keep on his lights after putting himself through school. Jeffrey and Ghislaine had already threatened to kill my loved ones, so I limited our phone calls, fearing that we were being monitored (Jeffrey had taken my flip phone and replaced it with a BlackBerry).

Back on the island, I felt more and more isolated. Ghislaine, Jeffrey, Jean-Luc, Sarah, and Nadia—the pyramid's top brass, in that order—had their own clique. They ate together, often away from us girls. Nadia spent a lot of time on her own around the island, and she certainly had no love for me. Among the new faces cycling through, I formed no alliances. Many weekends, I would sit out on the stone porch thinking, *Why do they even want me here?* My service to the inferno's lone client notwithstanding, I rankled everyone's nerves. That's how Jean-Luc weaseled his way in as my good cop. He was pleasant toward me. He also did something, on the eve of 2007, that flung open the door for this book.

Jean-Luc had his own clique of sorts. He and the quack psychiatrist who treated me were part of a circle of fellow conspirators, enablers who, either directly or tangentially, abetted the slaughtering of possibly hundreds. "If I were to do nothing," social justice advocate DaShanne Stokes once said, "I'd be guilty of complicity." By that standard, our society, which primes us to look past the offenses of certain assailants, bears responsibility for allowing Jeffrey's monstrous operation to churn on.

Dr. Deborah Tuerkheimer explains how such complicity happens. "Unbeknownst to us, we are shaped by a cluster of forces that I call the credibility complex," she writes in *Credible: Why We Doubt Accusers and Protect Abusers*. "These forces corrupt our judgments, making us too prone to both discount the credibility of accusers and inflate the credibility of the accused. The most vulnerable women experience credibility discounting at its most extreme, while men who are protected by greater status or position are the beneficiaries of massive credibility boosts." Within this complex, those receiving "credibility inflation"— the wealthy and the well educated—often carry on their crimes with few, if any, consequences. Observes Dr. Tuerkheimer: "Our society confers a hidden benefit on powerful men." It does the same for Oxford-educated Brits whose accents lend them eminence abroad and, at times, immunity. Still, if Ghislaine, even with her Queen's English, happened to be melanin blessed, she likely would have been handcuffed a decade ago. What goes for the white and wealthy does not apply to the brown and marginalized, notes Dr. Tuerkheimer. Intelligence and morality are assumed of upper-class Caucasians. When such traits are evident in those elsewhere in the caste system, the majority culture often expresses surprise, as in, "Wow, she's so *articulate* . . . such an exception to her race." An exception, or a survivor of credibility discounting? I would say the latter.

I don't assume that everyone in Jeffrey's life knew of his wrongs, and, in fact, I'm sure some did not. Association isn't grounds for an assumption of guilt, and many sadists—though not so much Jeffrey—may successfully hide their violations. I'm just curious about how the dozens around Jeffrey were simultaneously deaf and blind to what should have been blatantly obvious. Take the renowned French hairstylist, Frédéric Fekkai, whose salon team cut my hair while I was caught in this sick web. Jeffrey paid for my grooming (cuts then could cost as much as $750); Sarah and Lesley arranged the appointments. Others have given similar accounts.

Frédéric has made clear, in public statements, that he's horrified by Jeffrey's villainy. "Neither he, nor the current management team, had any knowledge of the incidents described and, in Mr. Fekkai's limited acquaintance with Mr. Epstein, he never witnessed any of the deplorable conduct that led to Mr. Epstein's conviction," a spokesperson said on Frédéric's behalf in a *Daily Beast* piece, "Epstein Flaunted Girls After His Arrest at Hair Salon for Stars." And though flight manifests show that he flew on Jeffrey's plane—with Ghislaine and Jean-Luc—his team says, "Frederic is disgusted and sickened by Epstein's activities, which no one was aware of in 2000 and 2002, when Frederic accepted a ride on his jet. Had he been aware, he would never have boarded that plane, let alone with his 5-year-old son, his son's nanny and his girlfriend at the time."

Yet there is a financial link between Jeffrey and the salon. According to the *Daily Beast*, "Fekkai's brand had received an influx of cash years earlier from a company backed by L Brands"—the retailer owned by Jeffrey's billionaire client, Les Wexner. Former employees at Frédéric's New York salon recall Jeffrey arriving with groups of young women to be serviced. This was *after* he had been registered as a sex offender as part of his 2008 conviction. By then, Frédéric's team says, he had sold his company and was no longer involved in the salon. Yet Jeffrey, not socially shunned because of his criminal record, remained a regular salon patron. "In between services, the women sat on Epstein's lap or stroked his hair—in full view of the hundreds of guests at Fekkai's 9,000-square-foot hair emporium," the *Daily Beast* reports. "'It was very out in the open,' one former employee said. 'Everyone knew.' 'He didn't give an eff,' another former employee said. 'He was coming in like he was running the show. He didn't care.'" Though Fekkai was unaware of Jeffrey's depravity, one would think the salon's team might have raised a brow at a registered sex offender with young girls in his lap. My hunch is that those who did were reluctant to blow the whistle. Perhaps that has to do with the previously mentioned bystander effect, as well as with Dr. Tuerkheimer's point: we often lend the male, the white, the affluent—and I'll add the well-coiffed—a credibility boost many of us are unconscious we grant.

Another prominent man who socialized with Jeffrey: Sergey Brin, cofounder of Google. I know this because I was there when Jeffrey hosted Sergey and his then fiancée, Anne Wojcicki, founder of 23andMe, for lunch on Orgy Island. Three other girls and I were at the table in a cabana on the beach. Two of them were Mia and Trina, the emaciated ballerinas, one of whom barely spoke English. I was drugged out of my mind on my powerful combination of drugs. Ghislaine had given strict instructions ahead of the gathering. "You are not to talk to the guests," she said—hence our places at the far end of the rectangular table, as well as our muted tongues. None of us spoke, not even to each other. I'm not certain why they even wanted us there. Why would they risk displaying their trafficking scheme? I have often wondered whether Sergey and Anne thought the scene strange. I hope they truly didn't. And even if they had, I do realize that, per social custom, one isn't inclined to confront a host with questions about why he's surrounded by a group of young, silenced girls. How I wish this couple would have noticed us. Our lives were at stake.

Others, from afar, disapproved of Jeffrey's behavior. They spoke up only after he was dead. A former air traffic controller in St. Thomas, Jeffrey's point of entry to the Virgin Islands, reported what he had witnessed to *Vanity Fair*, in "'The Girls Were Just So Young': The Horrors of Epstein's Private Island." Says the anonymous source: "On multiple occasions I saw Epstein exit his helicopter, stand on the tarmac in full view of my tower, and board his private jet with children—female children. One incident in particular really stands out in my mind, because the girls were just so young. They couldn't have been over 16. Epstein looked very angry and hurled his jacket at one of them." Observed another airstrip employee: "There'd be girls that look like they could be in high school. . . . They were always wearing college sweatshirts. It seemed like camouflage. . . . I could see him with my own eyes. I compared it to seeing a serial killer in broad daylight. I called it the face of evil." That evil came with an open palm. "The fact that young girls were getting out of his helicopter and getting into his plane, it was like he was flaunting it," this employee said. "But it was said that he always tipped really well, so everyone overlooked it"—hush money doused in the tears of innocents.

Jeffrey is in the grave, leaving, in his wake, a plume of mystery and outrage. How could this happen, some ask. How could we allow a sadomasochist to rape right under our noses and suffer little consequence? Our tendency, as humans, is to do what I have sometimes done in these pages, what I still often do from my deep hurt, from my imperfection: label predators as savage brutes, which is another form of othering. "Calling these people 'monsters' merely dehumanizes the dehumanizers," writes David Livingstone Smith in *Less Than Human: Why We Demean, Enslave, and Exterminate Others*. "Calling people monsters is a way of whistling past the graveyard, a way of reassuring ourselves that *they* are so very different from *us*. . . . Moral outrage comes cheaply. It is more difficult, and surely more valuable, to address those features of the human condition that precipitated the tragedy."

I have come to believe that the *potential* for dehumanizing lives within all of us, as evidenced in The Story of humanity. Most will never commit the deeds that Jeffrey and Ghislaine have, or even conceive of such horrors. Yet our collective saga proves that we can be conditioned to hate, in ways both measured and unthinkable. Pulitzer Prize–winning journalist Isabel Wilkerson notes this in her book *Caste: The Origins of Our Discontent*, in a stirring passage about the Holocaust. "Germany bears witness to an uncomfortable truth—that evil is not one person but can easily be activated in more people than we would like to believe," she writes. "It is easy to say, If we could just root out the despots before they take power or intercept their rise. . . . It is much harder to look into the darkness in the hearts of ordinary people with unquiet minds, needing someone to feel better than, whose cheers and votes allow despots anywhere in the world to rise to power in the first place. It is harder to focus on the danger of common will, the weaknesses of the human immune system, the ease with which the toxins can infect succeeding generations. Because it means the enemy, the threat, is not one man, it is us, all of us, lurking in humanity itself."

Jeffrey operated out in the open. Scores colluded, either by direct involvement or by turning their heads. Additional predators, history has taught us, are around the next bend: Hitlers, Stalins, rapists, mass killers, ethnic cleansers. There will also be more conspirators and bystanders. If we keep our gaze affixed on Jeffrey, a sole unrepentant rapist, we'll lose our way toward a larger purpose: the injustices, here and now, that we can work to rectify. "We must always take sides," said Elie Wiesel. "Neutrality helps the oppressor, never the victim. Silence encourages the tormentor, never the tormented." Elie also wisely noted this: "The opposite of love is not hate, it's indifference." When we raise our voices against wrongdoing—be it silent and systematic, bold and belligerent, on our shores or overseas, in our neighbors and in ourselves—we offer profound grace to humankind. We, in effect, give love to ourselves.

My spirit let out a primal wail near the end of 2006. During a New Year's trip to Ghislaine's island inferno, Jeffrey sodomized me on back-to-back days, leaning me over his massage table as I begged for mercy. Afterward, Ghislaine swooped in with a round of body shaming. As a treat, aka a carrot, I had been allowed to eat what everyone else was eating on that evening. Ghislaine, without expla-nation, just snatched away that meal and replaced it with my usual cucumbers and tomatoes. I decided then that I had to escape and looked first toward the place I'd always found freedom: the open water. *Perhaps I can swim off this island*, I thought as I stumbled my way from the bungalow. Maybe I could front crawl my way out.

The sun had lowered its lids. The stars stared down over me, watching, blinking hard, wondering what I would do next. I knew the distance to St. Thomas was less than two miles. By day, if I squinted from the patio of the main house, I could glimpse it just beyond Great St. James. I crept out to an area I hoped was in a sur-veillance blind spot and noticed a quad bike the groundskeeper had left unattended. I mounted it, struggling to stay on because my backside throbbed. I turned on the engine.

I knew not to drive to the main beach. The urchins would sting me paralyzed. I sped toward the farthest part of the island, up to a rocky cliff edge. I dismounted and peered out over the sea, ob-served the waves pounding their fists on the rocks beneath the sky's angry scowl. I hadn't seen sharks but knew they swam be-neath, feeding on squid and soon, perhaps, me. Strangely, that thought didn't deter me. I had survived hell. An ending beneath the waves, in my temple of tranquility, seemed a grace note in a life drowned out by melancholy. Death felt preferable, in the moment, to one more rape. I stepped toward the edge, tried to determine how I could safely make my way into the sea. A fall from that cliff would have killed me. I stepped forward. Tears flooded my face.

I had just begun inching carefully down the rocks when I heard a commotion. I glanced over my shoulder. Ghislaine and

Jean-Luc, along with two girls and Jeffrey's bodyguard, sped up on quad bikes. Ghislaine made her way toward me and placed her palm on my back. I sobbed as she ushered me back to firm ground. "It's okay, honey," she cooed. "Come with us." They had obviously seen me on the video cameras and raced there not to save me but to ward off the ensuing public relations nightmare if I had perished on or near the property. Malicious Ghislaine, suddenly Glinda the Good Witch, was there to secure her job. Back in the bungalow, on my bed, I swaddled myself in my sheets and wept. *Where are you, God? Please help me.* I had felt His presence, years earlier onboard a Greyhound bus, during the journey to my earthly father's home. On that bed, from my core, I called out to my heavenly Father, the one, the only one I knew might hear me.

That miserable evening, low as it was, birthed two unlikely gifts. First, Igor Zinoviev, Jeffrey's Russian bodyguard and trainer, years later confirmed my attempted escape. While that didn't ease the heartache of what I had experienced, it offset my credibility discount. It also soothed a sore spot long festering in my gut. When a wealthy Jo'burg prep-school boy once raped me in his backseat, I was silenced by the community. Igor's corroboration was his way of saying, "I believe you. I hear you. I witnessed it."

A second windfall came courtesy of Jean-Luc. At the end of that trip, he chirped "Happy New Year, Sarah!" and handed me a disc. "Why don't you take these photos as a memory of the week?" he said. I studied his face. *Does he think this feels like a holiday?* "Okay," I said with a shrug. I took the disc—filled with photos he had snapped of me and the other girls on that weekend, as well as pictures from an island-hopping trip he and Jeffrey had taken to meet a business associate—and stuffed it in my bag. Ghislaine and Jeffrey didn't know I had it.

Jean-Luc's act of daftness become my stroke of luck. Those photos, a few of which are included in this book, later proved I had been on Orgy Island. The pictures also contradicted what Ghislaine has claimed, that she had phased out of Jeffrey's world by late 2006. The year before, in 2005, a search warrant had allowed police to comb through Jeffrey's Palm Beach estate. Ghislaine, at that point, largely receded from public view. Yet here she sat in the photos, giggling alongside Jean-Luc on Jeffrey's island patio, very much in her role as female kingpin. Not only was she still in Jeffrey's life then, they stood shoulder to shoulder in their abominable crimes.

I'd been back in New York for about a month when Jeffrey made an offer. "I'd like to send you home to South Africa," he announced one morning at his New York mansion. The catch: I would need to recruit a "personal assistant" from local modeling agencies in Cape Town. That obviously meant he wanted a new lamb for his butchery. I was told I'd be paid five thousand dollars if I delivered a young woman. By then I had heard whispers from the other girls that Natalya had been paid exactly that sum to trap me. Jeffrey's offer seemed to confirm that. He also promised to arrange my visa and US passport. *Exhale*. Ghislaine, on my way out, gave me her usual ultimatum: "Unless you get down to 114 pounds and bring back a girl," she told me, "Jeffrey cannot get you into FIT." I nodded and boarded my flight, booked by Sarah Kellen.

I played along with Jeffrey's request, even as I clutched the strong conviction I still hold: I would not send another girl into the jaws of such a monstrous machine. I understand that other survivors, marred by their assaults and desperate to survive, felt forced into a different choice. Yet for me, recruiting another young woman—especially knowing that a kind of death awaited her—represented an uncrossable red line. I packed my Atkins bars, the only food I would live on for the next month. Africa beckoned. I had been home only once or twice since I fled at age fifteen, and I missed the people, the swirl of colors, scents, cultures, the water calling to me, the vibrancy of the Motherland. Jeffrey promised to keep in touch on the BlackBerry he had given me. "I need to be able to reach you at all times," he repeated. I only suspected it at the time, but I now strongly believe that the phone was his tracking device for me.

I stayed with my dad. Jeffrey and Ghislaine had already forced me to hand over his contact details. Ahead of my trip, and also while I was there, he rang my father. He charmingly introduced himself as a businessman and philanthropist and explained that he was helping me enroll at FIT. Ghislaine called as well. They both assured him they only wanted to help. That raised suspicions for my dad, who pulled me aside one evening. Why would this man be so generous? What did he expect in return? I stayed silent about the rapes, unwilling to jeopardize what I saw as my one shot at school . . . it felt so close. My essay was nearly complete. And though I had no intention of returning with a "personal assistant," I did then still hope I could somehow achieve the weight loss goal I now know was impossible for me. Also, my father had lost the right to hear my truth, because he had silenced me following my brutal sexual assault years earlier. And why would he believe me now if he didn't then? Even if I told him what was happening, he would remain unwilling—he may say *unable*—to financially support me. What were my options if I returned to South Africa? He wouldn't make space for me in his home, his heart, when I had survived rape and become suicidal at fifteen. He also would not embrace me at twenty-two.

I blamed myself for my predicament. I felt enormous shame at the quagmire I had become entangled in and feared my father would pile on more judgment. He'd always been disappointed in me, full stop. This would add an exclamation point to his original assessment. My stepmom's reaction reinforced my belief. When I had shown up in Cape Town wearing designer gear Jeffrey purchased for me, I overheard her say to another family member, "For the first time in my life I'm really proud of Sarah. She's making something of herself." I wanted to vomit, and if I had had more food in my stomach, I might have. Meanwhile, because of the diet I was on, I had to seek medical treatment for my kidneys, a physical ailment mirroring my emotional one.

I still have the emails I exchanged with Jeffrey's team during my time in South Africa. I reassured them I was visiting modeling agencies to find a PA. I wasn't. At Jeffrey's request—and in correspondence facilitated by Lesley Groff—I sent photos of my naked body, as proof I was dropping pounds. Lesley actually asked me to send these nude photos. That's why I am astounded at her claim since then, through her lawyers, that she didn't suspect trafficking. I was not "underage," yet I was still coerced and sexually assaulted by the pedophile who employed her. Lesley sent me this note while I was in South Africa: "Hello Sarah! The following is from Jeffrey: 'I'm surprised I haven't heard from you.'"

I returned to New York—without a PA, and weighing ten pounds more than Ghislaine and Jeffrey required—in late February 2007. When Ghislaine first saw me, she shook her head and muttered, "Look who's back . . . the fat cunt. I don't think you'll be going to FIT anytime soon." Jeffrey summoned me to his townhouse, made me strip naked in his lobby so he could "evaluate" my progress for his "records," and then reprimanded me for failing at both my missions. He declared me still obese, yet obviously found me pleasing enough to rape—which he did right then and there, in his foyer, with an attendant passing through. I moved back into Jeffrey's building on Sixty-Sixth Street because I had no place else to live. The assaults continued uncurtailed.

Jeffrey did not mete out his cruelties alone. As aghast as we may be, as a culture, at the terror he inflicted, the spotlight is now on Ghislaine, Jeffrey's main co-conspirator, as well as those who kept his pyramid in place—the many women who recruited; the assistants who booked cars and flights shuttling the victims around; alleged fellow rapists such as Jean-Luc who joined forces with Jeffrey; and the dozens who stood by quietly as this atrocity unfolded in clear view. Ghislaine's family and legal team have sought to present her as a compassionate figure rather than the groomer and assaulter I know her to be. No one can predict whether Ghislaine will ever be convicted in court. I can only pray that she will at last be held responsible by her fellow citizens. The onus is on us, as a global community, to move away from victim blaming, and use our energy to put predators behind bars. Rapists seldom stop raping. They are still human and should be regarded as such, even though they've robbed others of their humanity. They are also accountable. It is not just our prerogative to hold them liable. It is an insistence upon our shared decency.

11

Silent Mutiny

A stallion has various gaits. One is a walk, the steady clip-clop of hooves against the earth, the trampling and stirring of red dust. Another is a trot, faster than an amble, slower than a canter, the equine version of a jog. A galloping wild horse bolts across the grasslands, breathless and unbridled, neighing and leaping. My escape from hell, my freedom break, unfolded at all three paces.

The wandering and wondering happened first. Even before Jeffrey sent me to South Africa to recruit a PA, I began searching for an exit. Though Ghislaine and I had nearly finished my FIT application, I had an inkling Jeffrey would never help me enroll. I still wanted that with everything in me. In fact, I agreed to go to Cape Town only because I still hoped that it was possible. But deep down I knew it might not happen. So in between my shifts of pleasuring him, I rounded up freelance modeling gigs, trying to earn a bit of my own money. I also started looking for a true way out, one that would not jeopardize my life or my family's. A few weeks before I boarded my flight, a door cracked open.

I was roaming the Upper East Side when I stopped in at my usual corner bodega. Over the months I had befriended a homeless guy, an affable elderly man who knew all the locals. That shop and corner were his turf. Whenever I came through, I would give him a dollar or two, talk with him briefly until he began to chat up the next neighbor. He had often mentioned wanting to introduce me to a friend of his, a neighbor who had been especially kind to him. "You two should meet one day," he'd say, laughing. That day came just as I was leaving the bodega one Sunday morning. "Ah, Sarah," he said, "this is Dan!" He nodded toward a gentleman, handsome with a wide smile. We greeted. I blushed. He asked me out.

That was in late January 2007. Coffee became dinner became my total infatuation, one born, in large measure, of my desire to be rescued. I had fallen under Rick's spell for exactly that reason, and, frankly, I still hadn't gotten over the toxicity. Relationship wounds, like ancestral patterns, may lie dormant for a time but do not magically vanish. My longing for the Fairy Tale, for Barbie's dollhouse life, compelled me toward a patriarchal prince. Dan checked all the boxes: dashing and dimpled, with cheerful eyes; successful, with a top job at a bank; seemingly protective, and a decade older than me. I recognize now I wasn't in love with Dan. I was in search of a father and a savior.

I was also numbed out. I was already high on my cocktail of prescriptions, but I had craved a deeper paralysis, a way to tranquilize the pain that led me to that island cliff. Breathing, thinking, limping, even hoping . . . all of it throbbed. I had no money for coke, but I had stayed in touch with Gary Malhotra, the Quo nightclub owner Natalya introduced me to. (Incidentally, three years after I met Gary, a waitress in his club accused him of shoving her into a closet and attempting to sniff coke off her derriere. The *New York Post* reports that she filed a $3.5 million civil suit. Gary denies the claims. He was convicted of sexual abuse, harassment, and forcible touching in 2009.) Upon my return from the New Year's Eve trip, I called Gary. He gave me a gram of the big C, enough to quell my angst.

So when I met Dan through the homeless guy, I was half dead and looking for a new hero. I latched on to him with the iron grip of a fatherless girl, with the wish that he would care for me in ways no partner can. In those years, that's the imbalanced power dynamic I set up with men. For three weeks before I departed for Cape Town, he wooed me with evenings out at Michelin-rated restaurants, frequent calls, and flowers. My day job continued as Jeffrey's captive. My nights were spent in Dan's swish Upper East Side apartment. I told him about my FIT dream and Jeffrey's help with my enrollment. I said nothing of the rapes, the island. It was too early in our relationship, and too mortifying for me to utter. Still, I hoped that, upon my return from the Motherland, he might eventually become my passport to freedom. I also prayed Jeffrey would keep another of his promises—to arrange a visa for me to stay in the United States to study. Dan, fond as I was of him, could not offer me that.

Three weeks later, when I returned to the city, Jeffrey went apeshit. Not only had I failed to bring him a victim and drop the weight; I had also had my hair cut into an edgy style, with green hair extensions added throughout. He immediately sent me to

Frédéric Fekkai's salon, where my color streaks were removed and Jeffrey's preferred look was restored: wholesome, coiffed, muted. He also gave me an ultimatum. "If you keep resisting me like this," he spat, "I'm going to throw you on the street." I had known my hairstyle would have repercussions. And while I wanted to lock down my visa, I had also glimpsed, in Dan, a potential path from hell. That prospect gave me the courage to begin raising my middle finger in silent mutiny. This stallion was preparing to trot.

Jeffrey and I rowed constantly the next week. "You're never going to get me into FIT!" I screamed, with a fierceness that scared even me. "Well, I would if your fat ass would lose the weight!" he shouted before pinning me to his massage table. The initial immense fear I'd had of Jeffrey, the trepidation clasping shut my jaw, morphed into a rage that overtook my tongue. I got so aggressive during one fracas that he sent in Natalya again. "Everything okay?" she texted me. "Just cool off with Jeffrey. You'll get through this"—same song, seventeenth verse.

Meanwhile, Dan and I had picked up where we left off. Through tears one evening, after a massive brawl with Jeffrey, I told him, in vague terms—and still without revealing the rapes—the heartache I was enduring. He held me close and whispered comfort, said I should come stay with him. The timing turned out to be fortuitous. That week, Sarah sent a car to take me to Jeffrey's mansion for my usual once-a-day rape. With my emotions raw and my clitoris inflamed, I refused to go. Jeffrey, in a spite-filled rant over the phone, told me to get the hell off his property. I moved right in with Dan.

Jeffrey, however, wasn't done torturing me. "With this attitude you're giving me," he shouted on that call, "fuck, no, I'm not getting you into FIT!" Yet as he removed that carrot, he left two others dangling. He could still help me line up my visa, he said, as well as continue covering my prescription costs. The catch: I would need to remain on call to service him sexually, a few times a week in New York. I agreed in that moment but continued my trotting, because when Sarah next sent for me, I did not respond. A half hour later, as I was walking on Lexington Avenue, a black sedan rolled up beside me. Out hopped Jeffrey, who grabbed me by the elbow and pulled me into the back seat. "This'll teach you not to run from me," he hissed in my ear. My BlackBerry had indeed been a tracking device; that's the only way he could have known my location, unless he had had me followed. His driver, another deaf-mute bystander, stared straight ahead as I wailed. At the townhouse, Jeffrey raped me for what felt like hours. "If you ever try to run from me again," he murmured as he left the room, "I'll find you and fucking kill you. You will never escape from me, Sarah," he said. The stallion, the wild galloper, had other plans.

As I was quietly plotting my freedom run, Ghislaine, the effervescent gadabout, was living her best life. Judging by a stroll through the online database for Getty Images, the visual media company featuring a vast compendium of photo archives, Ghislaine was trading double-cheek kisses with the glitterati all throughout 2007, both while I was away in South Africa to recruit a PA, and after my return. By this time, Jeffrey was under scrutiny by the authorities. He had been for some time. In 2005, the Palm Beach police had stormed the pedophile's estate, finding lewd photographs of children (in one, a girl who appears to be age six is bent over with her backside exposed, reports the *Daily Mail*), and several of Ghislaine (she is outstretched naked on a beach in one picture, according to the same story). Then in June 2006, the summer before I was trafficked, a grand jury indicted Jeffrey for one count of solicitation of prostitution. That charge did not reflect that the victims were underage. The FBI opened its investigation. Perhaps Ghislaine's fellow bon vivants hadn't heard about the raid or investigation, but Ghislaine herself was well aware. And yet, on she mingled, grinning and clinking glasses, both in New York and overseas. Up to that time, she had paid little, if any, real price for her close affiliation with a brazen sadist. That would continue to be true for years.

Ghislaine's 2007 began rather swimmingly, soon after she had guided me away from that cliff edge on New Year's Eve. Weeks later, on January 27, she dashed across the pond to attend Andy and Patti Wong's Chinese New Year Party, the garish annual bash frequented by celebrities and royals, including Ghislaine's friend Prince Andrew. The event's reported dress code during the Year of the Pig: "burlesque, debauched, or Hollywood black-tie." That was just the start of her fraternizing. Days later, she was back in New York for a fashion collection party; a Valentine's Day tea; and on March 7, as Jeffrey was on the verge of kicking me out of his building, the NRDC Ninth Annual Benefit, honoring *Vanity Fair*'s then editor in chief Graydon Carter. The madam must have felt right at home. At the event with her was Harvey Weinstein, still ten years away from his first rape accusations. *Birds of a feather*.

Right around the time Jeffrey yanked me into the back seat of his sedan, Ghislaine hosted a soiree in her swank Upper East Side townhouse. By then, she was well known for her tawdry manner: she once threw a dinner party on how to give a blow job and placed dildos at each setting, according to the *Vanity Fair* piece, "'Ghislaine, Is That You?': Inside Ghislaine Maxwell's Life on the Lam." She was equally known for surveying a room for recruits. One holiday, per the same *VF* piece, she attended the party of a billionaire. "Oh, my God, look at those girls!" a friend heard her say. "I didn't realize that they're so beautiful! Can you introduce me to them?" The friend wondered aloud why she had wanted to meet the girls. Ghislaine replied, "I'd like to meet them because I know Jeffrey would like to meet them." That friend recognized, for the first time, a sinister motive beneath Ghislaine's socializing.

Her March 2007 home gathering, however, involved no raunch or apparent recruiting. She organized a celebration on behalf of London-based interior designer Allegra Hicks, grand-daughter-in-law of Earl Mountbatten, a member of the British royal family. A day later, per *WWD*, the celebration continued at Swifty's restaurant, then on Lexington Avenue—and steps away from where Jeffrey traced and abducted me before whisking me off to violence. Revelers at Swifty's included Tory Burch and her then beau Lance Armstrong; Renée Rockefeller (at the time married to Mark Rockefeller, son of former US vice president Nelson A. Rockefeller, who served under President Gerald Ford); and Valesca Guerrand-Hèrmes (then wife of Mathias Guerrand-Hermès, heir to the luxury French handbag company). Proximity is certainly not proof of knowledge, and none of Ghislaine's party-mates may have known of her role in a sex ring. My point is that Ghislaine did—and she continued sashaying about, with no sense she should lie low while the FBI was investigating her co-conspirator. What gall.

And what irony that Ghislaine, queen of the filthy mouth club—and a woman who once attended a "Hookers and Pimps" party with her friend Prince Andrew—seemed to get all puritanical when questioned about allegedly gagging and raping a victim with a sex toy. In her 2016 deposition, she was asked whether she kept a basket of sex toys in the Palm Beach house. "You have to define what you are talking about," she said at one point. "I don't recollect anything that would formally be a dildo, anything like that."

Perhaps she'd rather discuss hand puppets. In unsealed court documents from the settled civil defamation case between Virginia and Ghislaine, Virginia claimed that Prince Andrew once used a puppet to grope her at his townhouse in 2001. Virginia says Ghislaine was present during the alleged violation. A second woman, Johanna Sjoberg, has said Prince Andrew used the same puppet to touch her inappropriately. "I am not aware of any small handheld puppet that was there," said Ghislaine during her deposition. *Might she have been aware of a* large *one?* She rambled on: "There was a puppet—not a puppet—there was a—I don't know how would you describe it really, I don't know how would you describe it. Not a puppet, I don't know how you would describe it. A caricature of [redacted] that was in Jeffrey's home." Both Prince Andrew and Ghislaine deny the two women's accusations—and Ghislaine still says, with nary a stutter, that she knew of no sex trafficking ring, much less participated in one.

Alfredo Rodriguez, Jeffrey's former butler in the Palm Beach estate in 2005, said she at least knew where the funds were going. "Ms. Maxwell was like the lady of the house," he told the *New York Times* in 2019. Alfredo said that the house expenses were paid from an account in her name. He has also said, in a sworn testimony, that after the girls gave Jeffrey massages, he would wipe down vibrators and sex toys for his boss and put them away in an armoire near his bed. (In 2010, Alfredo was convicted of obstruction of justice and sentenced to jail for eighteen months, after he tried selling Jeffrey's alleged black book to an undercover FBI agent for fifty thousand dollars—and would not then give the journal to prosecutors. The *Miami Herald* reports that he told investigators he had seen nude minors at his supervisor's pool and knew Jeffrey was having sex with them. In 2015, he died at age sixty following a mesothelioma battle.)

In 2007, socialite Ghislaine was clearly glad-handing all over town—yet she later claimed that, during that period, she was backing away from her partnership with Jeffrey. It seems she was flying closer. Jeffrey paid for Ghislaine's training as a helicopter pilot, reported the *Daily Mail* in a 2019 exclusive. She received her pilot's license in 2007. Later, after Jeffrey had been granted his sweetheart deal and served a laughable jail term, he bought Ghislaine a four-million-dollar Sikorsky S-76C. "Records show that Epstein also had another helicopter, a Bell Jet Ranger, which Maxwell flew at his sprawling Zorro Ranch in New Mexico," reveals the *Daily Mail*. "The blue and white chopper has the tail number N491GM—GM standing for Ghislaine Maxwell—and was nicknamed Air Ghislaine 1." Her father once named a yacht for her. Jeffrey followed suit with a fancy chopper, a vehicle they used to transport victims into Hades.

Actress Ellen Barkin has taken issue, via Twitter, with Ghislaine's flight path. "Epstein's pimp girlfriend, Ghislaine Maxwell, a very well-connected Brit socialite cannot just walk free. . . . She pilots planes to and from the island. I know because she told me. She is a sex trafficker." While Ghislaine was learning to fly and continuing to groom, I was reeling, then trotting, then eyeing my deliverance.

St. Patrick's Cathedral spans a city block at Fiftieth Street and Fifth Avenue, right across from the hubbub of Rockefeller Center. The Neo-Gothic architectural marvel stands as tall as Big Ben, with twin spires soaring skyward. For nearly one hundred and fifty years, the seat of the Roman Catholic Archdiocese has flung open its majestic doors to popes and parishioners, priests and cardinals, the faithful and the faithless, sinners and strangers. On one spring evening it beckoned me onto a pew beneath its stained-glass windows.

This was on the day Jeffrey tracked me down, forced me to his townhouse and toward a new low. Hours later when he released me, physically chafed and spiritually leveled, my feet somehow carried me south. I walked to St. Patrick's a mile away, whimpering in the shadows as I shuffled down Fifth, avoiding the questioning stares of others. The bronze sanctuary doors stood open when I arrived. On a pew near the front, I dropped to my knees, cupped my face in my palms, and cried out to the trinity. *Help me.*

See me. Save me. Free me. For much of my life, I had roamed and ached, for my father, from the shame, for a grounding force more powerful than my smallness. The ambling, the sauntering, had rendered me lost. I had nowhere else to search and just one plea to make, that God, the Great Bestower, would grant me His favor. My entire existence had been that one prayer, a life, head bowed, in pursuit of His grace. I don't recall how long I knelt there weeping and distraught. But when my lids slid open in the dark, in the stillness, I sensed deeply an abiding presence, the inner knowing I've always felt.

Jeffrey sent for me a few days later. Dan, of course, protested my involvement with Jeffrey. What man wants his girlfriend being helped by another? I would leave soon, I assured him, I just needed that visa. I had purchased my own phone as a way to evade him yet had to keep his BlackBerry to receive his calls. He didn't rape me this time but rather handed me a paper. On it was scrawled the contact info of a top cosmetic surgeon, a friend of his. He had arranged an internship for me with the doctor, a position that would allow me to get my visa paperwork underway, the carrot he used to keep so many of his victims close. "He'd like to interview you," he told me. "You should call him and set it up." The next week I arrived early for the appointment, hair freshly blown at Fekkai's salon, dressed smartly in designer pieces, a facade of professionalism to disguise my despair. The eyes, however, betray one's brokenness. They speak, they shout, they groan, they mutter. They tell of a misery no couture can mask.

The interview went well. Near the end, the surgeon thanked me, asked if I could start the next Monday. I could. I walked out, shoulders raised, and feeling proud of myself, like I had turned a corner; I recognize, in hindsight, that the bend was still in hell. I walked straight to a possible modeling gig in the area, and while on my way there, my phone rang. It was Jeffrey. "You left your items in the surgeon's office, you stupid bitch!" he howled. I froze. "*What?!*" I squealed as I frantically rifled through my bag. *Oh my God. . . . It's missing.*

I had carried with me that day a brown A4 envelope, containing my modeling shots and a gram of coke. Somehow in my joy after nailing the interview, I had left it there by mistake. "I've phoned the police, and they are on their way to arrest you!" Jeffrey screamed, with no pause between each word. "We're coming to get you *now!*" *Click.* With quivering palms, I powered off the BlackBerry and took out the SIM card, with the hope that he could no longer track me. I scanned the corner—near, far, diagonal— and bolted up Madison Avenue, pumps scraping the skin from the backs of my heels, beads of sweat dribbling down my temples. I ducked into a Starbucks to catch my breath, darted out again, and peered over my shoulder. My feet, my heart, all pounded in unison, and every few paces, I craned my neck backward. Still, I kept galloping, through crosswalks, past bodegas, until finally, at Dan's place, I thrust open the door.

Dan was at work when I raced into the apartment, slammed the door shut, and locked every bolt. I quickly packed my belongings with one hand, dialed my mom and lit a cig with the other. "My life is danger, Mum," I said, my words tinged with terror. "You have to book me a plane ticket to London *tonight.*" Pause. "What the hell is going on, Sarah?!" she said. "I can't talk about it," I said, "but please, please, please . . . you've got to get me out of here now!" She said she had no money but could borrow it from Jack, the landscape architect and former beau still in her world. The soonest they could book me was on a flight the next evening. I thanked her and descended into sobs.

That was around 4 p.m. Dan, whom I called, raced home at five. I gave scattered details before melting into wails, and as he held me, we talked in hushed tones. I don't think I slept a full hour that evening; the next day I was even more paranoid. I paced and smoked, kept checking the deadbolts, felt sure that the NYPD would break down the door at any moment. That evening, Dan saw me off to my red-eye flight, and by nine, I was onboard, yet still terrified. I glanced to my left, to my right, behind me, looking for signs of Jeffrey, Ghislaine, the police. "Ladies and gentlemen," the pilot said over the loudspeaker, "we're next in line for takeoff." I sat back in my seat and closed my lids, drew in a long breath and held it. Only after the engines roared and we lifted from the earth did I slowly, tearfully, breathe out a silent prayer. *Heaven heard me.*

Part III

RESOUNDING

I write for those women who do not speak,
for those who do not have a voice because they
were so terrified, because we are taught to
respect fear more than ourselves. We've been
taught that silence will save us, but it won't.

—AUDRE LORDE

12

Hunted

I believe in ghosts. The haunting, the holy, the evil, the pure, my life is steeped in the supernatural. Some spirits burden. Others heal. And one phantom in particular boarded my flight from New York to London. I may have galloped from hell, heart palpitating and hair ablaze, yet the plume, the ashes, the ghost of paranoia, hovered above me, below me, inside me for years. At every turn I felt hunted. That is because I was.

I used the word *paranoia* for lack of a more precise term. While it describes the ongoing anxiety I mean to convey, it also means something that I do not: irrational delusion. What I and others have voiced feeling is based on a universe and experience quite real. We have been to an underworld few can conceive of, a Hades with its own distorted rules: left was right, up was sideways. And in that kingdom, even our instincts were gaslit. That's why I nodded in recognition when Maria Farmer once spoke of Ghislaine's arrest and detention. "Forgive me, after this giant conspiracy theory I've lived, that I don't believe anything," she said in *Epstein's*

Shadow, a 2021 docuseries. "I want proof. I'd like to see her. She may very well be in Trump Tower." In another interview, with *CBS This Morning*'s Anthony Mason, Maria, who had worked as a receptionist in Jeffrey's townhouse, said he once showed her a room filled with stacked monitors, and male spies watching them. "I saw toilet, toilet, bed, bed, toilet, bed. I'm like, 'I am never gonna use the restroom here and I'm never gonna sleep here.' . . . It was very obvious that they were, like, monitoring private moments." Maria's point aligns with mine: things are never as they appear in the shadowy Epstein-Maxwell Matrix.

That is partly why I stayed silent with my mother about what, exactly, I'd escaped. After I landed at Heathrow Airport in May 2007, Mum and Jack met me in the arrivals hall. My poor mother still hadn't gotten over the fright I gave her. "Oh my God, Sarah . . . what has happened to you?!" she said, hand over heart, as she burst into tears. She pulled me toward her, patted my back as we embraced, and then stood back so she could gaze upon the dreadful sight I was. At 122 pounds, I looked anorexic, with skin hanging from my upper forearms. My lifeless eyes sat atop dark, puffy circles. My face was covered in acne. My teeth were yellow, my voice unsteady. I reeked of fear and death. We hugged again as I sobbed, choking back the vileness of what I had survived, exuding utter brokenness.

I breathed not a word on the two-hour drive from London to Broadstairs, the seaside town in Kent where my mother was then living. Once we were there, Mum prepared a home-cooked meal, the whole time glancing at me and welling up. Over sausage and mash, she pressed me for details of what I had endured. "I shook my head as my lids filled with tears. "Don't ever, ever, ever ask me what's happened" is all I said. I refused to speak for two reasons. First, I knew if I told my mother the truth, it would break her, and she'd end up doing something that would get her killed. Jeffrey and Ghislaine were well connected not just in America but in the UK and well beyond. I feared for Mum's safety as much as my own, so I had to go underground for both our sakes. And, second, speaking of my enormous shame would have meant revisiting a torment I longed to bury. Both silences were meant to protect me. Neither fully did. I'd promised myself, on the plane to Heathrow, that I'd go to my grave with The Story. I didn't yet recognize that one's grave, one's death, can come while one is yet breathing.

I stayed at Mum's place for several weeks, but I knew I couldn't live there forever, nor did I want to. My mother, bless her, was still plagued with the same struggles, the same addiction to liquor that had landed her in the UK. Ancestral spirits linger that way. She also had no money and was barely making it on welfare benefits. I applied for job after job in London, mostly in administrative work. The last official full-time position on my CV was as a recruitment agent at a headhunting firm, all the way back in my Edinburgh days. I couldn't explain the gap in my employment history and still didn't have a degree. The rejections poured in, and with each, I felt more and more like a failure. I did all I could to come across as stable, happy, confident. I was none of the above. Perhaps those who interviewed me saw past the little show I put on.

"If you watch close," novelist Chuck Palahniuk once observed, "history does nothing but repeat itself." In my case, it bellowed the second time around, as I returned to a life I thought I had forsaken. Sexual assault had become so normalized for me. It's all I knew. The refrain that pulled me toward escorting years earlier again cleared its throat: *You are nothing . . . so you may as well get paid for your nothingness.* Any scrap of self-worth I might have had was rooted in my appearance, the one trait much of the world, and particularly men, seemed to value. We learn our worth, in part, based on how others perceive us and what, if anything, they prize in us. I called an exclusive escort agency and made an appointment for an interview. I got the job and went for a photo shoot.

My rate was £750 an hour, just over $1,000—far more than I could earn at any other job requiring no diploma. I often went home with thousands after just one shift, as the wealthy business-men I accompanied took me out for dinners in five-star restau-rants, dancing, a full evening. One client even flew me to Italy with him for two days, forty-eight hours times my hourly rate. It was *ridiculously* good money at times, all of it legal. I had my reg-ulars and each was respectful. Some appointments did not even involve sex; I can't tell you how many men simply wanted me to nod compassionately as they opened up about their marriage woes, shared things they felt they couldn't with their wives.

The agency's madam, Fran, was fond of me. I had briefly told her, in the most hazy terms, about the ordeal I had come through. She actually tried to talk me out of escorting, as she could see how traumatized I was. She also helped me find a room to rent, in the home of a lovely Indian man she knew. I stayed with Mum for a few weeks before I moved in with Rohan, an IT business owner in his fifties. I loved the idea of lodging off the radar, with no address in my name, and with a landlord who might step in to protect me if Jeffrey and Ghislaine sent a sniper. Rohan was a sweetheart when sober, and domineering when he drank. I, of course, latched on to him. From the day I moved in, we began a relationship. He and Fran insisted I stop escorting, which I did after a few months. So-called easy money—I was raking in five thousand dollars a week, minimum—comes with a steep emotional price tag; much as I loved the exorbitant pay, the wining and dining and Chanel bags, my self-worth further plummeted.

I had convinced myself I could handle escorting. I couldn't. Intimacy is designed to connect us on both the physical and emotional planes, and though some insist the act needn't create soul ties, my spirit said differently. Once I left escorting, Rohan hired me as his personal assistant. We were together for a year before our mirroring dysfunctions wedged us apart. By then, I had saved enough money to rent a semidetached house on Bollingbroke Grove in Battersea, south London, a place I chose because it was out of the way. The house sat opposite a cemetery, a resting place for the dead, staring down on one hardly living. I paid my rent in cash to avoid opening a traceable checking account, installed dead bolts, and hung blackout curtains. That was not paranoia. It was a recognition that, years later, was confirmed. Another survivor forwarded to me an email Jeffrey sent to her. It read, "hi, was Sarah Ransome a friend of yours?" I still have that creepy note, dated January 13, 2017, about a decade after I had fled the sociopath (and when I was pursuing justice for him in court). I didn't need such an email to know what I still do: once you've been caught in Jeffrey and Ghislaine's sickening cult, you can never again breathe easily. Jeffrey is dead. Yet his specter, the panic, remains.

That ghost spooked me in summer 2008. By then, Jeffrey was all over the headlines. On June 30, in a Palm Beach County courtroom, after victims in braces had testified to his depravity, he pleaded guilty to two charges that pointed a finger at his underage victims by referring to them as "prostitutes." He then received his joke of a sentence, that eighteen-month joyride in place of true jail. One great injustice, among many, is that Jeffrey's victims learned about his secret sweetheart deal only *after* its implementation. That is because Alexander Acosta, the US attorney for South Florida at the time—pressured by Jeffrey's powerhouse defense team, which included former US attorney Guy Lewis and former US solicitor general Ken Starr, the prosecutor who investigated Bill Clinton's sexual liaison with Monica Lewinsky—sealed the plea bargain. The number of accusers and their ages was thus hidden, as was the protection of Jeffrey's "known and unknown co-conspirators." Ghislaine has sought to use that shield to have her charges dismissed.

Shockingly to many but not to me, the government and Jeffrey's lawyers were apparently colluding, as attorney Bradley Edwards has noted. "The damage that happened in this case is unconscionable," he told the *Miami Herald* in 2018. "How in the world do you, the US attorney, engage in a negotiation with a criminal defendant, basically allowing that criminal defendant to write up the agreement?" Courtney Wild, represented by Bradley, concurs, and added another point. "As soon as that deal was signed, they silenced my voice and the voices of all of Jeffrey Epstein's other victims," she said.

The survivors filed an emergency petition asserting their right to be informed, per the federal Crime Victims' Rights Act, and fought to have the plea pact unsealed. A legal bloodbath ensued and ended with their triumph. Meanwhile, in a land far, far away yet ever closer, the headlines sliced opened a wound for me that hadn't ever healed. The news became a rape of a different sort, the destruction of the wall I had built around my emotions. "You can't ever stop your thoughts," Jena-Lisa Jones told the *Miami Herald*. She was assaulted by Jeffrey at age fourteen. "A word can trigger something. For me, it was the word *pure* because he called me pure in that room and then I remember what he did to me in that room."

I tried to turn off the telly amid such reports, yet found myself consumed with every trenchant twist and turn of the case. One weekend when I was visiting my mother, Jeffrey's smug face splashed onto the screen. I broke down and finally told Mum what had happened, though leaving out the most disturbing details. She'll learn things in these pages that I only now, almost fifteen years later, feel ready to share. That is how I know I love my mom: the mere thought of breaking her heart breaks mine.

In the recovery of your voice after years of muzzling, you may not instantly shout, or even murmur. First there is a cough, and then a mutter, followed by months of stammering, of fixing your tongue, your being, around unspeakable vulgarity. And then one morning, when you're curled up in a ball next to your mom, the rage, the blaring, pours forth. That is the process, the vocal adolescence, from silence to full resonance.

All of 2008 felt cursed. My Father Wound, and the familial pattern that helped form it, invited an unsettling spirit. Soon after I moved to Battersea early that year, Dan, the boyfriend I had lived with in New York, relocated to London for a job at a bank. I had a funny feeling about Dan. I still do. While he seemed to care for me, and he voiced anger at Jeffrey's abuse, he was never outraged enough to actually help me break free. Once when I told him I might go to the authorities, he said, "Why don't you just move on and forget this whole thing?" I wondered then if he was somehow conspiring with Jeffrey. They worked in the same industry, and Jeffrey had once been a client of his bank. I have no proof that they were connected. I just had a question mark lodged in my gut, the sort of inkling I've sometimes ignored at my peril—which is what I did when he called. "I've missed you *sooo* much," he practically sang. I fell for that rubbish, mostly because he was speaking a cacophony that fit with my life's discord.

He already had his own flat in London but asked if he could move into my place. I quickly agreed. Eager to halve my rent, as well as to feel a man's protection, I thought it was a great idea. It wasn't. We quickly fell back in lust, a distraction I welcomed amid the jarring Epstein headlines. I had lived with Dan for only two months in Manhattan, and it soon became apparent I didn't know him as well as I thought I did. His sordid fantasies disturbed me. I once snooped through his wardrobe and found a sword, next to a fantasy book on rape. When we were intimate, he wanted me to wear a strap and give him anal all the time. Maybe he was gay. Maybe he was bi. And, for sure, he was dismissive of my protests of that act. He was aware of my grievous history, just as my ex, Rick, had been. And that, I realize now, was part of the issue. My past, in their view, put out a welcome mat for perversion. Once they knew my full story, that narrative changed how they regarded me. I was no longer a princess on a pedestal. I was a nothing to be further violated. Looking back, I feel that what most pierces me is that I tolerated it. During those times, I believed I had no worth. I thus attracted men who confirmed that assessment.

Despite my misgivings about Dan, I stayed with him while moving on from escorting. I was hired at an aviation company that specialized in creating interiors for private planes, the last place I needed to be in light of my memories of the Lolita Express. But the manager, who undressed me with his licentious gaze during the interview, offered me an exit ramp from a job and lifestyle I needed to move on from. Meanwhile—I told you 2008 was a bear—my mom was brutally attacked by a tenant she had taken in as a way to lower her rent. I'd awakened that morning with a sixth sense she was in trouble and rang her. She was in the hospital being treated for injuries. I rushed to see her, and then went to her place to collect her things. The house looked like a crime scene, with furniture turned upside down and blood splattered on the walls, carpet, mattress. The lodger, unbeknownst to Mum, was mentally ill. A psychotic break prompted him to beat her nearly to death. After her hospital release, I could not let her return to that space. I temporarily moved her in with Dan and me. I gave Mum my bedroom, and he and I slept on an air mattress in the spare room.

If three's a crowd, four's a heart attack. "Phantom Epstein" floated above our trio, with TV anchors and tabloids hurling fresh daily triggers throughout that summer and into fall. Also, there were now *two* alcoholics in the house. My mother's drinking was out of control; mine wasn't far behind, and came mixed with the prescription drugs I had stayed on because I'd formed a habit. So I, the inebriated, was looking after Mum, the smashed, which put me back in my role as her caretaker at a time when I needed support. I kept tabs on her around the clock. When I glanced away, she'd end up in some dodgy pub. One night when she went missing, Dan and I drove around Battersea for hours. We found her stumbling down a dark road, with her shoes hanging off her feet as she tripped along.

Around then, a work trip turned devastating. My colleagues and I flew to Atlanta and San Francisco. The journey started with hugs and high-fives among the team, the excitement of taking the brand abroad. It ended with me pinned down by a stranger . . . another sexual violation, another vulnerability resulting from my drunkenness. I had gotten so wasted that evening that, upon staggering back to the hotel, I entered the wrong room. The man inside, high on crystal meth, took advantage of my state and raped me. I somehow got away, and later scrubbed my flesh raw in the shower as I bawled. If I had been a wreck before I left London, I returned on the brink of breakdown. Jeffrey's plea deal and its attendant PTSD, Mum's alcoholism and our crippling codependence, the spirit of bedlam invading everything—

the cumulative weight sat down on my chest and left me gasping for air.

On August 16, three days after my birthday, I fully choked. Dan had forgotten my special day and made amends by taking me to lunch at Bluebird in Chelsea. He also bought tickets for the film *Mamma Mia*, as a treat for my mother and me. "I just need to pop home and pick up a present I got for you," he said, smiling, as he dropped us off at the cinema. He asked if he could use my house keys because he'd misplaced his. *Sure.* We agreed that he would meet us at a cocktail bar a couple of hours later, after the show. He pecked me on the lips and drove off.

Mum is agoraphobic. The crowded theater prompted a panic attack, and we stepped out halfway through the movie and headed early to the bar. I rang Dan but his phone was off. *Hmm.* I tried him over and over, but every call went to voicemail. I wondered aloud whether he'd been in an accident. "But then why would he power off his phone?" Mum said. *True.* One hour turned into three, and finally, my cell rang. I picked up with fear in my throat. "Are you okay!?" I asked. Pause. "I'm fine, Sarah," he said. Longer pause. "What the hell is going on, Dan?" I said. He dryly explained that he had moved all his belongings out of my place and never wanted to see me again. *Click.*

Mum and I, pissed as parrots, raced home by cab. Since Dan had taken my key, I had to ring a locksmith. "Ma'am, I can't let you in the property unless you can prove you live here," he said, lifting a brow at our drunkenness. I lost it. There I stood, unable to get into my one safe place, my sanctuary, after a man had just cruelly abandoned me. I had no driver's license or ID bearing the address.

I finally reached my landlord, who vouched for my tenancy. Once inside, I suffocated. The agony of the previous months, a lifetime of sorrows, strangled me with such force that I gagged and spit. I stumbled toward the bathroom, opened the medicine cabinet, emptied the contents of every pill bottle into my palm, and left the apartment, wailing. Mum was passed out on the couch.

When I had attempted suicide at age fifteen, I wanted attention. This time, I wanted to die. I shoved the capsules in my mouth all at once, heaving and choking as they tumbled down my throat. Amid the havoc, I butt-dialed my boss without realizing it. He sensed something was wrong and drove to my house. Mum, still out of it, told him about the evening, and said she didn't know where I was. He raced out to search and crossed paths with a neighbor who was walking his dog. "Have you seen Sarah?" he asked, describing me. The guy pointed toward the cemetery across the street. "I think I saw someone climb over that wall," he said, shrugging. My supervisor dashed toward the graveyard while calling an ambulance. There, in the pitch-black, behind a tall tombstone at the rear of the cemetery, I was curled up in a fetal position and weeping quietly. I did not want to be found. I wanted to join the departed.

When I was rushed through the ER doors, my heart had already stopped. Doctors shocked me back to life with a defibrillator and pumped my stomach. I had thirty-seven seizures and lay in a coma in the ICU for four weeks. I also had pneumonia and contracted MRSA. The photo in these pages captures my state. My mom rang Dan and told him I'd tried to kill myself. Mum says he swaggered in holding a newspaper, took one look at me, and walked out. He did not speak or show emotion. He just left me for dead. And while I was unconscious, another blow: my grandfather passed away.

Time, it has been said, is a great teacher. It instructs most adeptly, I believe, when combined with clear-eyed introspection. In those years, I clung to my woe-is-me story. I saw the world, and myself, through that lens. *Misfortune always finds me*, I'd think. *I'm so unlucky*. That's why it cut me so deeply that Dan left me, destroyed me, undid me . . . on and on. "Oh, how *dreadful!*" I wanted others to acknowledge, with their palms over their hearts. "I can't believe what you've suffered." Thirteen years and much self-examination later, I know better. I see more clearly. I understand what I couldn't at age twenty-four, when I was blinded by my own narrative of misery, crying not just a river but an entire ocean. On that evening, I lost my way and might have missed life's master class, if the Father had not spared me yet again.

From here, miles beyond that mayhem, I look back and see my hand in creating it. What Dan did was inhumane. What Rick did was equally horrific. I mourn the heartache. I also see how, without knowing it, I invited their mistreatment, made the abuse comfortable, asked it to stay for tea, shoved down the whisper that told me not to allow Dan back in my world. That does not exonerate either man. They're as accountable for their behavior as we all are. It does, however, leave me standing in the only place from which all personal power flows: ownership of my choices, my patterns, my inherited wounds. You can spend decades bemoaning your fate. I've walked that dead-end road. The path of growth for me began with a forceful recognition: I am the common denom-

inator in my story, the protagonist directing every scene and unseen, even if unwittingly. All plotlines, all threads, begin and end
with me. I woke up from my coma, confused about where I was,
and with years to go before I stepped into that awareness.

My hospital release marked the end of one season and the start
of another. The house was a mess. My body ached. I crawled my
way to the bathroom and into bed. Still, I asked my mother, who
drank herself into nightly blackouts, to please find her own place.
I could not nurse myself back to life while standing guard over
hers. She packed everything and left with hardly a goodbye. Two
years would pass before we spoke again.

My mother moved on, but the ghost of paranoia still floated above
me. As toxic as my relationship with Dan was, I had grown used
to having a man around. It eased my fear that, at any moment,
even in the wee hours, Jeffrey or his conspirators might suddenly
attack. I varied my routine, so that if a PI were following me, he or
she could not predict my schedule. I can relate to Jason Bourne,
the character played by Matt Damon in the film series. Jason, a
CIA assassin afflicted with amnesia, doesn't know who he is, how
he arrived in his situation, or where he's headed. He lives in fight-
or-flight mode, ever ready to wield a gun, convinced he's being
traced and targeted. That is how I felt for a decade after breaking
out of the Epstein-Maxwell horror show. Terror trailed me. In the
years after I fled hell, I have moved forty-seven times: to various
continents and countries, in place after place within cities, and
always—*always*—peering over my shoulder.

Even those on the outskirts of the sex ring have sometimes sensed they needed to watch their backs. Lady Victoria Hervey, the English model who briefly dated Prince Andrew in 1999, attended Jeffrey and Ghislaine's dinner gatherings over the years; she and the socialite were friends. In 2019, she told *Good Morning Britain* about an unnerving experience she had when she once visited the couple in New York. She'd come to town for a modeling job and stayed in one of the financier's apartments. "I did feel very uncomfortable staying there at the time," she said. "I cut my trip short, I felt like I was being watched, like there were cameras, hidden cameras." Her instincts were likely spot-on, given the rows of monitors Maria Farmer saw in Jeffrey's townhouse. "I left after about ten days or so and moved in with a friend of mine," she says. Lady Victoria, like each of us, was born with a sensor. We can feel when we're being observed. Our spirits serve as antennas.

Virginia Giuffre sensed eyes on her after escaping Jeffrey and Ghislaine. She'd been recruited by the socialite in 2000, she has said in court documents, while working as a changing room assistant at Donald Trump's Mar-a-Lago club. She had been sexually violated as a child, in and out of foster care, and homeless at age thirteen. The bubbly Brit promised to help her become a masseuse and earn lucratively. The trap was set. During two harrowing years in captivity, Virginia says Ghislaine and Jeffrey raped her constantly; loaned her out to Prince Andrew (who made a widely panned denial of her claims in a 2019 BBC interview); and requested that Virginia have a baby for them.

Virginia was clever. She convinced her captors to first allow her to get her massage certification—a carrot they had long dangled—and they agreed. Soon after, they sent her to Thailand for a massage course and also asked her to recruit another victim. While there, she met and married Robert Giuffre, an Australian who was visiting Thailand. When Virginia rang Jeffrey and told him she wasn't coming back, the pissed pedophile yelled "Have a good life!" and hung up. She settled into marriage and motherhood in Australia, with one eye always scanning the horizon. For years, there was no sign of Jeffrey—until 2007, after the FBI turned its sights on him. "Epstein calls me, and he goes, 'There's this stupid investigation going on about me, you know, and . . . are you going to talk to people about it, have you talked to people about it?'" recalls Virginia in the 2020 documentary *Surviving Jeffrey Epstein.* "I was, oh my God, like, I . . . couldn't sleep for days. I was just living in constant fear."

She's not alone. Bradley Edwards, who represented Virginia and more than fifty Epstein-Maxwell survivors, understands their heightened sensitivity. "Those who crossed paths with [Jeffrey] believed he was able to do anything, at any time, to anyone," he writes in *Relentless Pursuit: My Fight for the Victims of Jeffrey Epstein.* "I don't think I met a single witness who didn't believe they were being followed or investigated by him. And what made their paranoia reasonable was that, many times, they were right." Just when you think you can exhale, you receive a spine-tingling reminder, as I did via email, when Jeffrey asked a similarly uneasy survivor if she knew me. After that note showed up in my inbox, I reclenched my jaw and redoubled my efforts to stay underground. *Forever hunted . . . and haunted.*

13

Voice Lessons

"S hame needs three things to grow exponentially in our lives: secrecy, silence and judgment," says resilience researcher Dr. Brené Brown, author of *Rising Strong*. In 2016, the year I first gave voice to The Story, I abruptly cut off shame's water supply.

My throat clearing came on the heels of various silences, some more obvious than others. After coming out of a coma, and coming to grips with the fact that I could not be Mum's savior, I got a ping on my phone from an old flame. Years earlier, just before I had left Edinburgh for America—and after I had split with Rick—I went out briefly with Henry, a day trader with short dark hair, a little extra around the tummy, the look of an English aristocrat. We clicked immediately. As fond as I was of him, I was even more keen on my reset a world away. Still, when my phone lit up with a text message from him near the end of 2008, my heart lit up as well. We picked up right where we'd left off, and right in line with my Prince Charming hope. A couple of months after we began seeing each other, I gave up my London life—*what life?*—and moved in with him and his children, then twelve and fourteen, in a lovely cottage in the English countryside.

Henry had recently endured an acrimonious divorce. I thought he had worked through his deep hurt. He hadn't. It manifested as his attempt to mold me into an ex-wife he clearly had not moved on from. "I'd love to see your hair long and blonde," he said with the hint of demand in his voice. His ex had been platinum with flowing tresses. Soon enough, I had traded my black bob for goldilocks extensions, a look that was all wrong for me. He also liked his women submissive and would not allow me to work. "Darling, you don't need a job," he'd say, drawing me in for a hug. "I'll take care of you." Music to Barbie's ears, but trouble for her status in a relationship. Money is power, and whoever has it—be it in the open marketplace or in, say, a marriage—holds the reins. Still, I truly cared for Henry; his gentle manner offset his domineering tendencies. I predictably turned myself into his Stepford Wife, cooking, cleaning, and creating a beautiful home. His feast-or-famine income was initially all bounty, enough to cover our Aston Martin, holiday-home-in-Portugal lifestyle. But when famine balled its fist, it struck with great force. We went from vacations abroad to counting coins to buy groceries. To get through it, I drank, which also eased the haunting of a past I kept secret from Henry. I not only gave up my voice in that two-year relationship. In 2010, I left without a single pound—and with a fifteen-thousand-pound car debt Henry had financed in my name.

Pennilessness shoved me back toward codependence with my mother. We hadn't spoken since she moved out of my place in

London. I rang and sheepishly pleaded for a lifeline. She let me come stay with her in Ramsgate, a seaside town about two hours east of London.

I vowed I would never again use survival sex to stay afloat. I've since kept that promise. I cobbled together a living by taking on three waitressing jobs. Mum kept me upright with home-cooked meals and much encouragement. Though she was still struggling with alcoholism, I appreciated her support during this period. A few months into balancing plates and paying off debt, I reconnected with a classmate who had worked on a yacht. My spirit sat up straight as he described the adventure: a life onboard luxurious boats, serving the wealthy and sailing the region, with great pay, and room and board covered. *Sign me up.*

I was hired by a Russian couple, with a yacht based in northern Italy, a forty-five minute drive from Monaco and the South of France. I put my things in storage, packed two bags, and flew to Nice. As a full-time stewardess among a friendly crew of five, I made three thousand euros a month, and believe me, I earned it. During sixteen-hour shifts I served up decadence: lobster, foie gras, caviar, truffles. When I wasn't waitressing, I was polishing cutlery and Hermés ashtrays, Hoovering every inch of the boat, detailing toilets with Q-tips, starting all over right after I'd just cleaned. And if I never precisely fold another towel or linen, I will have done my share in this lifetime. We traveled from port to port all over the Mediterranean, with a day off here or there to sightsee. It was exhilarating, even if exhausting, and I felt grateful for the work. I loved waking up in Sardinia, marveling at the sun rising over the ocean. Another favorite was the Amalfi Coast. I enjoyed that life for a couple of years until another call beckoned near the close of 2012.

I had longed to be closer to my father, emotionally and, at that point, geographically. *What if he had allowed me to live with him when I was fifteen?* I would daydream. *How might my life have turned out differently?* In place of an answer I had a desire, to set aside my disappointment and give our relationship a chance. I had saved up money with my yachting work and knew I didn't want to live in Ramsgate, near Mum. I love London, but too pricey. I missed my homeland nearly as much as I did Dad, so I decided to move to Cape Town. I broke the news to mixed reaction. My father was happy, my stepmom less so, probably because she thought she'd end up paying my way. That didn't deter me, nor did it turn out to be true.

Whatever Dad and Linda truly thought of my move, they were gracious enough to let me stay with them for a month. I made a great connection soon after. I was sitting at the outside bar at the Bay Hotel in Camps Bay when a Harley-Davidson pulled up beside me. The driver—tall, tanned, and lanky—flashed a big smile at me. I noticed passengers getting off his bike and paying him. "Are you offering rides?" I asked. "I sure am, lady," he said grinning. "Would you like to book one?" *Um, yes.* I had just finished the series *Sons of Anarchy*, about a group of renegade motorcyclists, so his vibe piqued my interest. The next day's ride became the start of a friendship, a first for me with a man. I joined David and a group of bikers for a drive through Hout Bay, along the infamous Victoria Road, winding our way around Table Mountain. I relished the freedom, the wind running its fingers through my hair, the sun kissing my cheeks, the coast at my side. Only the sea knew of my shameful past. That is how planned to keep it.

I carved out a life, if implosion can be called that. My brother, still in Jo'burg then, helped me get a car. Bless you, James. I took a job in a call center for an international online casino. I hated it. There I sat, struggling with my own alcoholism whilst hastening the downfall of gambling addicts. My home life exacerbated the sorrow. I dated and then shared a place with Paul, a drug addict with a violent temper. Black eyes became my new normal. He once accused me of cheating, forced his hands down my jeans, ripped my panties off, and shoved them in my mouth. My un-voiced trauma didn't save me from heartache. It served as a mag-net for more of it. I grew furious when intoxicated, got thrown out of restaurants, resembled Mum more by the shot glass. First ache, then drink, then make poor choices—I felt powerless to get off that hamster wheel.

Dad and I improved our relationship to some degree. What kept me going through most days was knowing I'd see him once every couple of weeks for a family dinner in his home. We prat-tled on about nothing in particular, and never about my time in America. He and my stepmom frowned on my friendship with an unconventional Harley rider, not to mention my romance with an addict. Though my father still did not help me financially, I'm thankful he carved out time to see me. That is what I have always wanted . . . to be seen by him. If you had asked me then about our relationship, I would have said I wished he had pulled me closer. On this side of AA, I recognize how my drunken outbursts blocked intimacy. He and my stepmom were as embarrassed by my behavior as they were by those in my orbit, people, like me, on the fringes. And moving nearer to me then would have meant setting oneself ablaze. It's only once you're sober that you realize the trail of destruction you've left behind. I grieve the loss of the bond that might have been. My actions were an appeal for my dad's care, a voice, a plea not well disguised.

Two years into my time in South Africa, I lost my job. My brother lent me money. David, my Harley mate, let me join his business, taking tourists out on journeys all over Cape Town— one of my life's greatest joyrides, second only to yachting. David and I absolutely loved working together; we spent so much time onboard his bikes that he jokingly began calling me the monkey on his back. The gift of his friendship helped me stop drinking, an effort most difficult in a town known for debauchery. I became a twelve-stepper, realized that, yes, I had become powerless to all manner of Merlot—yes, I needed a Power greater. As I got sober, I turned to weed. I often hear pot smokers declaring that marijuana isn't addictive. I can assure you it was for me. Following sobriety, I spent another year moving on from weed. At least I wasn't also still drinking, ranting my way around town.

Much as I loved the Harley business, earnings were unsteady. David and I ended up living together, platonically, and that put a strain on our friendship. We prioritized the latter and so ended our business relationship. I went out on my own in the biker tourism industry. That was a disaster. The field is male-dominated, and my experience was too limited. I ended up broke and homeless, and my dear brother sent money for food. Meanwhile, my father and stepmom, who knew of my situation and lived in the most affluent area of Cape Town, owned a holiday home that sat empty. My previous drunkenness notwithstanding, that refuge that went unoffered cut deep. I felt like an outsider in my own tribe. In December 2015, Mum booked me a ticket back to the UK—and toward a season when The Story would open its throat.

My stay with my mother lasted the length of my pinky finger. I was stewing in resentment at Dad and suffering from major weed withdrawal, and hence irascible. Three days in, Mum and I rowed, what about I cannot recall. What I do remember is that she called the police, and I was escorted from her place with my bags and twenty pounds to my name. The cops dropped me off in the middle of Ramsgate. I called one of my cousins in London, and he invited me to stay with him for a few weeks. I didn't have enough money for the train ticket but wrangled it in King's Cross station upon arrival. I was surrounded by family on Christmas Day—he and some of my other relatives hosted me—and thankful to be embraced. My cousin and a friend helped me rent a one-bedroom apartment in a lovely town called St. Albans, about an hour north of London.

As I settled into a stability a long time in coming, my gaze shifted online in the spring. On EliteSingles.com, I connected with Peter, a Brit living in Barcelona and managing his own small investment firm. On paper, he looked like a left-brainer; online and in life, he was quick-witted and creative, emotionally supportive, slender with a thick brown mane, and, of course, more than a decade older than me. That Father Wound does not go quietly. Our phone conversations flowed effortlessly, and he flew to London so we could meet. We've been inseparable ever since. Among the merry-go-round of men who have cycled through my life, he's been the most steady. And yet, for months in the beginning, I withheld my humiliation. I feared that its revelation might shift his view of me, as it had in the past. Most of all, the great shame I felt was what kept my lips sealed.

In the spring of 2016, I went to stay with Peter, yet I kept my place in St. Albans; our connection was too new for me to uproot, in light of what I had given up for Henry. Barcelona is one of my favorite cities, bustling with a vitality that reminds me of home, and also populous enough to grant me anonymity, as one face in a sea of millions. Peter and I spent long afternoons getting lost in the crowds of Barrio Gótico, biking in the Ciutat Vella district, ducking into cafés for long conversations, savoring the sounds of flamenco wafting through the streets. And then, in autumn, the music suddenly stopped.

Hillary Clinton and Donald Trump were headlong into their presidential runs, in the lead-up to one of the most consequential US elections in modern history. Clinton, in her second bid to become commander in chief, and with the prospect of making history as the first woman in the Oval Office, had been perceived as the front-runner for much of the campaign. Trump, the real estate mogul and political neophyte, had clearly touched a nerve with his "America First" message and his branding as a blue-collar billionaire. The contentious campaign dominated the headlines, transfixing not just a polarized nation but the entire global community. The onslaught of press on those two candidates, each one with known ties to Jeffrey or Ghislaine, stirred in me a repressed rage.

Bill Clinton was part of Jeffrey's social circle. The pedophile had photos of the president on the walls and often boasted of their friendship, a reminder to me of Jeffrey's proximity to power and his willingness to use it for harm. "In 2002 and 2003, President Clinton took a total of four trips on Jeffrey Epstein's airplane: one to Europe, one to Asia, and two to Africa, which included stops in connection with the work of the Clinton Foundation," reads a statement issued in 2019 by a Clinton spokesperson. The president categorically denies any knowledge of or involvement in "the terrible crimes Jeffrey Epstein pleaded guilty to in Florida some years ago, or those with which he has been recently charged in New York," the statement says. The president also said that he had never been to Little St. Jeff's, a claim contrary to the memories of Virginia Giuffre and Steve Scully, an IT contractor who had once worked on the island. They reported their recollections in the 2020 Netflix documentary *Jeffrey Epstein: Filthy Rich*. Virginia said that, while she had dinner with Clinton on the island, she never saw the president do anything improper.

Shared plane rides prove nothing, nor can Bill Clinton's alleged presence on the island be photographically verified. What is clear, however, is that Ghislaine was at Chelsea Clinton's wedding on July 31, 2010. Bradley Edwards, who was representing Virginia in a civil case against Jeffrey at the time, says that Ghislaine had been subpoenaed for a deposition, but she then claimed, at the last moment, that she had to leave the country, with no plan to return, because her mother had become ill. Imagine Bradley's surprise when he spotted a photo of Ghislaine among Chelsea's wedding guests in Rhinebeck, New York (a spokesperson for Chelsea Clinton has said that she didn't become aware of the "horrific allegations against Ghislaine Maxwell" until 2015).

Trump has also appeared cozy with Jeffrey and Ghislaine in years past. In addition to calling Jeffrey a "terrific guy" in 2002, the billionaire and his then girlfriend, Slovenian model Melania Knauss (née Knavs), spent time with my traffickers at Trump's Mar-a-Largo property (the four are pictured together in a photo taken in 2000 at the Palm Beach club). Trump, like Bill Clinton, says he didn't know that Jeffrey and Ghislaine were serial rapists. He has also said that he and Jeffrey had a "falling out" years ago. As for Ghislaine, Trump would go on to mention her from the White House podium in 2020, after she was arrested in New Hampshire. "I haven't really been following it too much," he said of the case. "I just wish her well, frankly." He notably extended no such warmth to her scores of alleged victims. And then there's the reporting by journalist Michael Wolff, in his 2021 book *Landslide: The Final Days of the Trump Presidency*. He writes that Trump suddenly took an interest in Ghislaine in a conversation about whom he should pardon. "Has she said anything about me?" Michael claims Trump wondered aloud. "Is she going to talk? Will she roll on anybody?" What I wonder is why the president was even curious about whether she would spill secrets.

That whole October brought surprises. On the seventh, the *Access Hollywood* tapes were leaked, with Trump bragging to Billy Bush, "And when you're a star, they let you do it. You can do anything. . . . Grab 'em by the pussy." The same day, WikiLeaks began publishing emails from Clinton campaign manager John Podesta, with excerpts from Senator Clinton's paid speeches to Wall Street. Then, near month's end, on the twenty-eighth, FBI director James Comey sent a shudder up the world's spine when he reopened an investigation into Clinton's private server. All those frights preceded Halloween.

My blood curdled at something else. Whenever Donald's and Hillary's faces flashed on my screen, I didn't see an *Apprentice* star and a policy wonk, a red- or blue-state candidate. I glimpsed a man who once hobnobbed with my oppressors, and a woman married to a former president who befriended my assailants. Donald and Bill had dined with the predator who had sodomized me. My weeping at the sight of Donald and Hillary flowed from a visceral place, a spiritual basement where I had stored the wailing. I went from Peter's fun-loving girlfriend to one sobbing for no apparent reason. My reaction surprised even me. I began having flashbacks of my abuse, experiencing it all over again, frame by frame.

"When something reminds traumatized people of the past, their right brain reacts as if the traumatic event were happening in the present," notes Dr. Bessel van der Kolk, author of the groundbreaking book *The Body Keeps the Score: Brain, Mind, and Body in the Healing of Trauma*. "But because their left brain is not working very well, they may not be aware that they are re-experiencing and re-enacting the past—they are just furious, terrified, enraged." At one point, I was so angry that I kicked in our bedroom door. If I walked into our living room and the telly was on, I would become inconsolable. Peter would stare at me with eyes that said, *Why is this girl freaking out?* I now realize

The Story was preparing to speak. Those images triggered the first gags.

My fury intensified a few days later. I read a news story on the links between Donald Trump, Bill Clinton, and my abuser. The story pointed out *New York* magazine's reporting: that Trump attended a dinner party at Epstein's home. Also, according to federal tax records, Jeffrey donated twenty-five thousand dollars to the Clinton Foundation in 2006—the same year Jeffrey was arrested. I had nearly burst a blood vessel by the time I reached the end of the piece. The writer concluded that the true number of Jeffrey's and Ghislaine's victims may never be known. . . . The figure could be staggering, far higher than any we might fear. *Boom*—that notion pummeled me in the gut.

Not long after that spike in blood pressure, Trump's and Hillary Clinton's faces appeared on the TV screen. *How can they even be candidates?* I thought. Trump and Hillary's husband, Bill, had clinked glasses with my captors, with a woman who allegedly threatened to feed one of her victims to an alligator, with a man who forced children to perform oral sex on him. And yet there stood my assailants' acquaintances, grinning as they delivered their stump speeches. *Jeffrey and Ghislaine must be exposed.* Perhaps the real number of Jeffrey's victims would never be known, but the world needed to hear The Story of at least one of them. That evening, while Peter held me, I finally found the courage to speak my horror.

That article lit a fire in me that couldn't be doused. A few days later, I was still so incensed that I reached out to the journalist who wrote the piece. I explained that I wanted to come forward with my account of having been trafficked and raped. I also told her I had video evidence of public figures participating in Jeffrey and Ghislaine's pedophile ring. I didn't. I said I did because I was absolutely terrified that, once I went public with my story, Jeffrey and Ghislaine would find and kill me. I wanted to send them a message via the press: if you wage war on me, I will return fire by releasing my evidence. That would be my leverage, my way of protecting myself.

Jeffrey and Ghislaine didn't know whether I had videotapes, just like they couldn't have realized Jean-Luc Brunel had been foolish enough to hand me that disc. Still, it was a mistake for me to claim I had videos, though I did know that Jeffrey kept a trove of surveillance on every person who had ever visited his properties. He had once shown me footage when we were in his office, while he forced his fingers inside me as I sat on his lap. I felt desperate to be heard, to have the world acknowledge the savagery of Jeffrey's and Ghislaine's actions, to unsilence the screams of hundreds, if not thousands, of girls and women on multiple continents. I should have simply presented the photos and stories I've shared in this book. That truth is disturbing and convincing enough.

Initially, the journalist seemed interested in my story, and we began setting up a call. But then she went quiet. Shortly after, I realized that I was being followed by two men; they hung around every building I emerged from. I know when I'm being stalked, and this went on for days. I was sure that Jeffrey and Ghislaine had tracked me down again. I have no idea whether there's a connection between my emails with that journalist and the arrival of those men. Yet I knew my traffickers could get to me anywhere, anytime, in any manner they saw fit. They had often told me they would murder me. I believed them.

That's why I had to get the hell out of Barcelona. I've always found great comfort in the presence of animals. Peter booked a horse-riding holiday for us, deep in the Catalonia countryside. We stayed in a farmhouse, where the owner cooked us beautiful meals. Out on horseback, in the morning dew, I could breathe for the first time in months. At the end of our three-day stay, I dreaded returning to Barcelona, so we asked the owner if he knew of a nearby city where we could find an apartment. "Funny you should ask," he said. "There's a guy renting his house in a tiny town called El Mas de Bondia"—in a region known as Montornès de Segarra. Within days, it would become my sanctuary.

I went deep into hiding, created my own witness-protection program. I hired a company to pack up my St. Albans place and have my belongings shipped. Peter closed out his Barcelona home, and we signed a new lease together. I was in no emotional state to work, so Peter supported us on his modest commissions. (He had just one client then, so money was tight. Mum and my brother sent help when they could.) Only about fifty families lived in the historic village, built by Knights Templar settlers and perched on a hill. No one spoke English. Neither Peter nor I knew a word of Spanish or Catalan. We resorted to hand gestures when shopping at the market, and the people met us halfway. It's remarkable how much warmth can be expressed without words. The villagers, observing how little money we had, dropped off fresh vegetables on our doorstep.

Even once I was off the grid, The Story, awake and roaring, refused to be silenced again. I had read in the news about Virginia Giuffre's 2015 defamation lawsuit against Ghislaine. I admired Virginia's courage in stepping forward and knew her trial date was scheduled for the next spring. Peter encouraged me to reach out to her. In my quest to remain untraceable, I had gotten rid of my phone and laptop and was using Peter's. I no longer even had a bank account. Peter researched who was representing Virginia. That led us to Paul Cassell and Bradley Edwards. I contacted them at the end of October 2016.

That call changed everything. From the beginning, I made clear my mistake with the journalist. They appreciated the forthrightness. "Is there any way I can help with Virginia's case?" I asked. *Possibly*. They arranged for me to speak to her full legal team on a conference call soon after. With tears cascading down my cheeks, I shared The Story in searing detail, more of it, I'm sure, than they needed to hear. When you squelch your truth, you embark on a half-life, one depleted of oxygen, one suffocating as it limps and moans. You're not aware of just how little air you're taking in. It's only after you raise your voice that you realize you've been holding your breath for years. To live a falsehood is to stumble through the world in a permanent state of inhalation, with no ability to express, to feel, to sing, to experience. You are alive, yes, but not fully present. The quality of your existence is diminished by your voicelessness.

Virginia's team was astounded by the evidence I presented. It's rare for a survivor to have photos and emails corroborating his or her account. I had both, though it took some time to get my hands on all of it. When you move as much as I did in those years, you're fortunate if you still have your head, much less files and pictures from nearly a decade earlier. I searched through all the boxes that had been delivered from St. Albans. No luck. *Where are my two purple file boxes?* I had mentioned their existence in my email to the journalist. I was beyond distressed when I rifled through every single box and found . . . no purple folders. I still wonder how those items vanished.

And then, among my belongings, a miracle: in some unlabeled box I thought was filled with memorabilia, I spotted the disc of photos Jean-Luc had handed to me on the New Year's Eve trip. I also found a hard copy of a picture of myself, wrapped in a towel on the island pool deck, right before Ghislaine forced me to pose naked as she body-shamed me and clicked photos. A search through my old computers surfaced correspondence with Sarah Kellen and Lesley Groff. My story, noted Brad, seemed similar to the accounts he had heard from so many other survivors. He later found my initials listed in multiple flight logs for the Lolita Express.

My evidence had to be further vetted. Bradley and his law firm partner, Stan Pottinger, flew to Barcelona to meet with me and to authenticate my photographs and emails. I was a ball of nerves beforehand, pacing, trembling, frightened that maybe *they* were working for Jeffrey and Ghislaine. In the upside-down reality I lived, that wasn't a far-fetched idea. Our conversation began tentatively in a hotel conference room; it turned into a marathon spread over two days. I trusted Brad and Stan. Just as we can sense when we're being observed, we can intuit when we're in the presence of integrity.

Incidentally—though I don't think arbitrarily—Brad had two near-death experiences on that trip. The first involved an explosion onboard what was supposed to be his transport bus at the airport terminal in Barcelona. The bus was struck by a luggage transporter. When it flipped over, three people were killed and others were critically injured. Brad, mercifully, had boarded a different bus. Then in Fort Lauderdale, Florida, his home base, there was a mass shooting at the airport on the day of his arrival to the area. He just so happened to fly into Miami, a rarity for him. Coincidence? Maybe. Yet there's the very real possibility that Jeffrey and Ghislaine could have been behind these occurrences. They threatened my life continuously during my time in hell. Brad was surely on their hit list, because he had proved that he would stop at nothing to bring them and their conspirators to justice. To this day, he's still devoted to that mission.

That was in January 2017. In February, I flew to New York to serve as a witness in Virginia's defamation case. If you have never been deposed, I can recommend more pleasurable ways to spend a day. Over seven tense hours, I sat across from Ghislaine's attorneys, who seemed to relish tripping me up, pushing me to confirm names, dates, and painful memories I had long kept buried just so I could function. The process is intimidating. It's certainly not victim friendly. It rouses painful emotions that have lain dormant for years. Yet the forced catharsis, uncomfortable as it was, lifted a burden for me. My truth was out there, raw and resonant. My shame could not survive.

14

Ground Shifts

Freedom is habit-forming. After standing in my truth for the first time, I yearned to straighten my spine and tower even taller. I had spent a lifetime hiding my trauma and its attendant shame. By lifting my voice, I lowered my shoulders and stepped into a serene version of myself. I craved more of that liberation. It didn't come easily.

My outspokenness initially appeared promising. After my deposition for Virginia Giuffre's case, the lawyers submitted my affidavit, a signed document of my sworn claims against the accused pedophiles. In it, I testified that in 2006 and 2007 I had been lured into Jeffrey and Ghislaine's rape pyramid scheme and forced into sexual relations. I wrote that Ghislaine, procurer of underage girls and young women, "appeared to be in charge of their activities, including what they did, who they did it with, and how they were supposed to stay in line." My evidence showed that Jeffrey was still actively recruiting and trafficking victims at the very same time he was under federal investigation for assaulting underage girls at his Palm Beach mansion. It also placed Ghislaine at the photographic center of a sex ring at a time when one would think she would fly her copter below radar. In June 2017, with the benefit of my corroborating account, Virginia was able to settle her case—a de facto win.

The deep gratification I felt in openly sharing The Story prompted another step into the light. In January 2017, while I was still preparing for my deposition—and ten days before the statute of limitations on my assaults was due to expire—Virginia's team guided me in preparing my own litigation. I will always be thankful for the support and legal prowess of my attorneys, David Boies and Sigrid McCawley. In the lawsuit they and Bradley Edwards helped me prepare, I alleged that Ghislaine coerced me into providing sexual massages to Jeffrey on his private island and in his New York mansion. I also made clear that both she and Jeffrey threatened to physically harm me and destroy my career if I didn't comply with their demands. The horrors I've shared in these pages formed the basis for those claims, which I stand by— and which my evidence lends credence to.

The filing marked the start of a grueling two-year process. First came the familiar fear, the heart palpitations at the recognition that a sniper may lurk on any rooftop. Then came that email, passed to me from another survivor, with Jeffrey's unnerving question: "hi, was Sarah Ransome a friend of yours?" I couldn't sleep for weeks after reading that message. I sank even lower underground. I stopped nodding and smiling at locals, fearing that one might be a mole. I wouldn't even register with a physician because doing so might have revealed my whereabouts. For long stretches I yearned for sunlight as I hid indoors. After more than a year of full sobriety, I reached again for the bottle. I had no access to an AA community in a remote Spanish town, and also no desire to be seen publicly even if I had. I just sat in the house, hour after hour, biting my nails and topping off my wine glass. Mine was no simple open-and-shut case. There were dozens of ebbs and scarce flows, long periods of waiting until we could appear before the judge or get endless rounds of paperwork signed and submitted to the court. For every step forward, we took a dozen backward. The delays felt unbearable, particularly since I had nothing else to occupy my dragging afternoons. I was a mess. Peter was a mensch.

And then we entered "discovery," the phase during which all parties exchange information in preparation for trial. Documents are demanded. Interrogations ensue during depositions. While I had already been deposed in the previous case and didn't have to suffer that hot seat again, the torment extended beyond me. The defense team said that they might subpoena my mom and brother, my dad and stepmother, and every man I'd ever dated, including Peter. If they had been able to subpoena the doctor who delivered me in South Africa, I'm sure they would have tried. Some of the potential witnesses could offer no testimony helpful in elucidating my attackers' behavior. Relevance was not the point. As Sigrid and Bradley explained to me, a rash of subpoenas is sometimes threatened as a form of legal intimidation. Ghislaine and Jeffrey were well aware I had irrefutable photo and email evidence, strong enough to trounce them in court. Better to scare me off than to have me disclose my documentation in court, their team may have reasoned. At every turn, they did all they could to get my case dismissed. When that didn't work, they resorted to vigorously shaking my family tree.

My father's throat tightened at the possibility of a subpoena. "No way can I get involved in this," he said. *Conversation closed.* He and other family members were so afraid they would become ensnared that some cut me off on social media and stopped answering my calls. Mum supported me, while my brother expressed misgivings. Honestly, I felt protective of them all. Despite our challenges over the years, I care about my family. And my father and I were on speaking terms then, after a lifetime of seesawing between cold shoulders and vitriol. I refused to put us back into a standoff. Though I wish my dad had at least given lip service to his support of my speaking up, I understood why he and others didn't want their names affiliated with the most notorious sex-trafficking ring of our times. Not only would that be a legal nightmare; for the Macphersons in particular, members of the British peerage, it would tarnish their proud legacy. "Me Too" sounds reasonable until it visits your doorstep. My need to stand in my truth—to leave behind my great shame and possibly send two prolific predators to prison—was less important than maintaining appearances. Still, I couldn't blame my loved ones. Jeffrey and Ghislaine had repeatedly threatened violence. No one can be faulted for ducking out of the path of a bullet. Their involvement might have invited their end.

The desire to protect one's tribe is a leading reason many victims of sexual assault tend not to raise their hands and voices. RAINN (rainn.org), a widely respected advocacy organization seeking justice for sexual assault survivors, cites evidence that most sexual assaults go unreported to police, with two out of three kept quiet. Those figures align with reporting trends globally. Two other reasons that survivors often bury their dreads: fear of retaliation and a belief that the authorities will not meaningfully intervene. And the vast majority of perpetrators, reports RAINN, will never see the inside of a jail cell. That leaves them on the streets, raping with impunity for sometimes decades, as former USA Gymnastics doctor Larry Nassar did. Our world has confirmed time and again that even when victims—and particularly female or marginalized ones, those most subject to the aforementioned credibility discount—speak up, their wounds are often minimized; their stories are discredited; and the stigmatization costs them their livelihoods. When gymnast McKayla Maroney told the FBI she had been assaulted by Nassar, she says the phone went silent before one of the agents blurted out, "Is that all?" McKayla says the agency took a year and a half to document her report, and even then, it was riddled with falsehoods. "They allowed a child molester to go free for more than a year and this inaction directly allowed Nassar's abuse to continue," she told the Senate Judiciary Committee in September 2021. Simone Biles, the greatest gymnast of all time, male or female, testified alongside McKayla. "The scars of this horrific abuse continue to live with us," she said, adding that "the impacts of this man's abuse are not ever over or forgotten."

Even survivors who brave the litigation process are subject to the same credibility discounts that govern our views outside the courtroom. "The ready availability of certain stock representations of lying women makes it easy for us to disbelieve," writes Dr. Deborah Tuerkheimer in *Credible: Why We Doubt Accusers and Protect Abusers*. "One figure who looms large is the 'gold digger.' Within the legal system, plaintiffs of all kinds can be questioned about their financial interest in bringing suit, and lawyers who represent accusers in civil cases are well versed in this line of attack. But sexual misconduct accusers are even more susceptible to such treatment than others."

Sexual assault victims in particular, observes Dr. Tuerkheimer, are often seen as those seeking an easy payday. "Sex crimes prosecutors must also contend with the 'gold digger' stereotype, which the defense can deploy in criminal court," she notes. "At Bill Cosby's retrial on sexual assault charges after his first trial ended in a hung jury, Cosby's lawyer said of the accuser, 'What does she want from Bill Cosby? . . . Money, money, and lots more money.' Outside the legal process, accusers are besmirched in the same way. One study of how Twitter users respond to sexual assault accusations against high-profile men found that users frequently selected the hashtag '#golddigger' to digest their reactions. The gold digger desires fortune above all else; if need be, she will even concoct an allegation of abuse regardless of what she must endure when she comes forward."

My ultimate choice to settle was about ending the carnage. By the time I waved the white flag of surrender, the protracted legal massacre had already cost me my calm and potentially might have cost my loved ones their lives. In the fall of 2018, Ghislaine's defense team said that if I didn't accept their settlement offer, they would definitely subpoena my tribe. Checkmate, and I relented.

I had dreamed of facing Jeffrey and Ghislaine in court. I was all geared up to go to trial and, in so doing, give a voice to the hundreds of Epstein-Maxwell victims who are too scared to speak. But after two years of a process that left me wrought up, I settled to end my hell. My attorney and I celebrated the outcome as a triumph. The real victory for me—child of a father who once only half-acknowledged (with wilting sunflowers) my rape, target of a schoolboy whose wealthy parents purchased my silence—was simply in being heard. Even without a trial and a verdict, my claims had been aired. If I had it to do over, I wouldn't change a thing. It was worth the restoration of my voice. My settlement came with no gag order, no further way to silence me. I'm free to speak openly about the heinous acts committed, to implore the world to put predators behind bars so that they cannot carry on raping. I have given myself over to that calling.

Throughout my discovery process, Ghislaine and Jeffrey were almost certainly in touch. They had clearly stayed connected throughout Virginia's litigation. The two exchanged emails in January 2015, according to court papers unsealed in 2020. In one note, Jeffrey appears to be offering his co-conspirator the language she should use to defend herself amid accusations of sexual impropriety. He writes: "Since JE was charged in 2007 for solicitation of a prostitute I have been the target of outright lies, innuendo, slander, defamation and salacious gossip and harassment . . . false allegations of impropriety and offensive behavior that I abhor . . . and have never been a party to. . . . I have never been a party in any criminal action pertaining to JE. . . . At the time of Jeffrey's plea I was in a very long-term committed relationship with another man and no longer working with Jeffrey. Whilst I remained on friendly terms with him up until his plea, I have had limited contact since . . . I am not part of, nor did you have anything to do with, JE plea bargain. . . . I reserve my right to file complaint and sue for defamation and slander."

In response, Ghislaine writes, "I would appreciate it if shelley would come out and say she was your g'friend—I think she was from end 99 to 2002"—in reference to Shelley Anne Lewis, the hedge fund manager's alleged secret girlfriend for three years, reports the *Daily Mail*. It seems Ghislaine sought to make clear that she had no romantic involvement with Jeffrey during that period. Jeffrey replies, "ok, with me." He also writes, "You have done nothing wrong and i woudl [*sic*] urge you to start acting like it. go outside, head high, not as an esacping [*sic*] convict. go to parties. deal with it."

And she did party on, until her rumba, like mine, abruptly halted. Back in 2012, around the time I was scrubbing toilets onboard a yacht for the wealthy, Ghislaine was flouncing around Manhattan, decked out in a floor-length floral dress at the Time 100 Gala: Time 100 Most Influential People in the World, held at Jazz at Lincoln Center on April 24, and posing alongside Martha Stewart at the American Made Awards at Vanderbilt Hall on October 16. She also tried to blot out her history as an accused rapist by turning over a new professional leaf. That same year, she founded the TerraMar Project, an environmental charity, and two years later, she gave a TEDx talk on ocean conservation. "Ms. Maxwell disappeared from the social scene after 2015, the year that Ms. Giuffre filed the defamation suit against her," reported the *New York Times* in 2019. "By 2016, Ms. Maxwell was no longer being photographed at events. That April, the New York townhome where she had lived was sold for $15 million. By 2017, her lawyers were saying that she was in London but that they did not believe she had a permanent residence." On July 2, 2020, the day Ghislaine's crimes finally caught up with her when the FBI broke through her front gate in New Hampshire, the socialite's new address became the correctional center where she awaited her own legal reckoning.

If living my truth was a spiritual exhale, ending my litigation proved a salt bath for the soul. Near the close of 2018, we moved just outside Sitges, a charming Catalonian town on a reserve smiling over the sea. Nature, again, soothed my senses. In the quiet following the tempest, I had mixed emotions. I was relieved the case was settled, but also wistful at not having my day in court. Amid the quandary, I soaked in the stillness.

In the spring of 2019, Senator Ben Sasse, a member of the Senate Judiciary Committee, called and asked me if I would be willing to testify against Jeffrey, in support of the government's case against the financier. *Absolutely.* Just before that conversation, I had come across an article about Jeffrey's Avenue Foch apartment, in Paris's Embassy Row. There, he had reportedly hosted Israeli prime minister Ehud Barak, Steve Bannon, Prince Andrew, and Bill and Melinda Gates (before their union ended amid speculation that Melinda disapproved of Bill's ties with Jeffrey). In France—with its history of granting a wide berth to the likes of filmmaker Roman Polanski, who had fled to the country after being indicted in Los Angeles for drugging and sodomizing a thirteen-year-old girl—the legal age of consent is just fifteen. (Legal consent ages vary around the globe: thirteen in Japan; fourteen in China, Germany, and Italy; fifteen in North Korea; sixteen in the United States and in my home country, South Africa, as well as in much of the world; eighteen in Kenya and India; twenty-one in Bahrain; and in Iran and other Middle Eastern countries, one must be married to engage in intercourse.)

"Did you know that Jeffrey has a home in Paris?" I asked Senator Sasse, though it was more of a statement than a question. I mentioned France's legal age of consent, adding, "I can assure you he's not going there for the wine and stinky cheese." I was astounded that the American government, knowing all that it had learned under the eye of Geoffrey Berman, the US attorney for the Southern District of New York, would even allow Jeffrey to leave the country, much less visit the cradle of erotic pleasure. "He goes to Paris so he can legally recruit fifteen-year-olds and rape them," I said. Senator Sasse may have been less than amused at the eye roll in my tone, but I was eager to get my point across: Jeffrey regularly took his predation to countries where he could operate with the greatest ease. When he bought Orgy Island way back in 1998, he was purchasing noninterference: tropical isolation freed him to indulge his deepest perversions away from the limelight.

On July 6, a few short weeks after that conversation, I arose early one morning, made myself tea, and turned on the telly. "Jeffrey Epstein has been arrested on sex-trafficking charges," said a reporter. I lowered my teacup and turned up the volume. "The financier was apprehended upon his arrival from France to Teterboro Airport in New Jersey," the journalist continued. "Epstein is expected to appear next week in Manhattan federal court." *Oof.* Some moments glide past without much notice during our lives, while others press their thumbprints deep into our flesh. This one bore down hard and held its position, leaving me with an indelible mark, a profound impression of both exhilaration and disbelief. "Peter!" I yelled, leaping from the sofa. "He's going to prison!"

Peter dashed into the sitting room, question mark on his brow, and we stood, spellbound, as the news unfolded. I could not believe it. I still can't. This man had evaded justice for much of his life, and now he was in custody. Just the idea of him in an orange jumpsuit, at last chastened and possibly incarcerated for the rest of his days, prompted a waterfall down my cheeks. *Jeffrey will never be able to rape again.* When I first came forward with The Story, I thought I had fully breathed out. This news brought a greater sense of liberation, as if a boulder had been lifted from my being. I still tear up just recalling it. I hadn't realized how all those years of hypervigilance had robbed me of peace, of the ability to slide back in a chair. I had lived with the stress, the static betwixt even life's high notes, that Jeffrey could destroy me at any time. And then suddenly, astonishingly, he no longer could. The Jeffrey who could get to me, the billionaire with unparalleled access and connections, was now inmate 76318-054. *Thank you, heaven.*

That news unfolded in slow motion, in contrast to the frenzy that followed. The press churned out hourly stories on this prolific rapist whose enormous web spanned North America and Europe,

Asia and Africa, and perhaps unknown nether regions, with victims who may take their screams to the grave. *Where was all this coverage when Jeffrey was raping girls in Palm Beach?* I thought. What a difference two decades make. Since then, the cultural landscape has shifted dramatically, with the times still changing even as we're standing in them. The seismic cultural accounting, the aftershocks of Me Too, the toppling of powerful men including Roger Ailes and R. Kelly, chef John Besh and cult leader Keith Raniere—time is most definitely up. The change was too long in coming, but I pray that it's here to stay.

After pleading not guilty, Jeffrey, an extreme flight risk, was denied bail, thanks to the pleas of survivors Annie Farmer and Courtney Wild. *Phew.* Jeffrey, the maverick who had lived above the law, reportedly sought to create his own rules and creature comforts in the vermin-infested Metropolitan Correctional Center in Lower Manhattan, the facility where Mexican drug lord Joaquín "El Chapo" Guzmán has been housed. The *New York Times* reports that Epstein hired several lawyers to visit him in jail for as many as twelve hours a day, which meant he could consult with them in a conference room rather than remain in his dank cell. He also gifted other inmates with deposits to their commissary accounts, his way of staving off potential assaults. But he couldn't buy his way out of apparent misery. On July 23, after being denied bail, Jeffrey was found in the fetal position on the floor of his jail cell, with marks on his neck. Prison officials couldn't determine whether the injuries were self-inflicted, yet he was put on suicide watch (though some in the press have reported that he was taken off suicide watch about a week after that incident). On

August 10, thirty-six days after Jeffrey was arrested, I awakened to another thunderbolt: my rapist was dead. Upon hearing that he had hanged himself, my elation morphed into devastation. I am not prone to fainting. Yet I collapsed and drifted in and out of consciousness, chest heaving each time I came to, bawling so hard I emptied myself of tears. *How could this have happened?*

While I initially believed the reporting that Jeffrey committed suicide, I am now among those skeptical that Jeffrey killed himself—and not just because it's plausible that many in his black book would have good reason to want him dead. He had video footage of some of the world's most powerful men engaged in despicable acts, and if that evidence had ever seen daylight, entire industries and factions of government may have fallen as swiftly as I did upon hearing of Jeffrey's death. The suicide story is riddled with coincidences that do not appear coincidental to me. First, the video surveillance from Jeffrey's earlier possible suicide attempt was inadvertently erased. *Hmm.* And we are supposed to believe that the two surveillance cameras in the hallway near Jeffrey's cell *both* happened to malfunction on the night of his death? I'm quite dubious.

And then there's the report from the Office of Chief Medical Examiner of the City of New York, which ruled the death a suicide—in direct contrast to the findings of Dr. Michael Baden, the forensic pathologist brought in by Jeffrey's brother, Mark. "There were fractures on the left, the right thyroid cartilage and the left hyoid bone," Baden said on *60 Minutes*. "I have never seen three fractures like this in a suicidal hanging." The two prison guards who were supposed to check on Jeffrey slumbered at their desks (they were both working overtime; they were also later charged with falsifying records). They admitted to that charge and eventually reached a plea deal with federal prosecutors. The guards' last check was at 10:30 p.m. Shortly after 6:30 a.m., the guards found him in a kneeling position, with his sheet wrapped around his neck and tied to the top of his bunk. CPR did not revive him. He was removed from his cell and rushed to New York-Presbyterian/Lower Manhattan Hospital before his body could be photographed. He was then pronounced dead a short time later. An ending, yes, but also the start of an enduring mystery—one eerily similar to the scandal hovering over Robert Maxwell's death. Ghislaine's plotline, too, shows pathologies repeated.

Jeffrey is gone, and with him, a full accounting of his misdeeds and motivations. We may never know what happened in his cell in the wee hours of a midsummer morning. I know only that we survivors were denied justice. Even in his death, he eluded responsibility. If he took his own life, he chose the coward's way out. And if he was murdered, then his prey, the multitude of us, were robbed and ravaged once again.

15

Heart Speak

August 27, 2019, will forever be bookmarked in the pages of The Story. It's the day I moved from prose to pathos, when I spoke not just from my intellect but also from my core, that place from which all spirit flows. The transition from girlish to full-throated, that deepening of my voice, took place in a federal courthouse. Had it not been for my neighing inner stallion, the experience would not have occurred.

Soon after Jeffrey's death, my legal team mentioned that Judge Richard M. Berman, who presided over *United States v. Jeffrey Epstein*, had invited victims to share their stories in a New York City courtroom. "Mr. Epstein's death obviously means that a trial in which he is a defendant cannot take place," the judge would later say. "I believe it is the court's responsibility, and manifestly within its purview, to ensure that the victims in this case are treated fairly and with dignity." *Bless you, Your Honor.* "I'd really like to be there," I told one of my lawyers. The line went quiet. "Well I think it's only for US citizens, Sarah," I heard. Cue the neighing. That was the end of our conversation but certainly not the end of the matter.

My attorney was kind enough to put me in touch with Wendy Olsen Clancy, the victim witness coordinator at the United States Attorney's Office for the Southern District of New York. She was arranging the hearing. I phoned and explained how important it was for me to attend, to raise my voice alongside those of other survivors. Same refrain: Americans only. "But that's nonsense," I said, "because there are so many victims internationally. Jeffrey raped girls and women all over the world. I've just successfully come through my court case against Ghislaine. I truly want to be there." Silence. "All right," Wendy finally said, perhaps sensing I was not to be deterred. "Let me see what I can do. Call me back in a couple hour's time." Two hours later on the dot, I rang her. "We've agreed to allow you to come," she said. I pressed the phone closer to my ear. "Really?" I said. "Yes," she said, chuckling. My travel expenses would even be covered, she said, as my heart leapt into a hula dance.

Peter traveled with me. He had been at my side throughout my evolution, from my silence to those opening stammers. It was only fitting that he'd also stand with me during such a defining experience. I had been consumed with every twist in the Epstein-Maxwell case since I came forward in 2016. But I still hadn't had my day in court. And while Jeffrey supposedly lay buried in an unmarked Florida grave, and Ghislaine was on the lam, my assailants needn't be present in order for me to take back my power.

We flew in on a Monday, the day before the hearing, and checked in at Hotel 50 Bowery. The FBI had arranged for survivors to stay there, five minutes by car from the courthouse in Lower Manhattan. I had already prepared my comments, memorized and rehearsed them ad nauseum. In school growing up, I excelled at speechmaking, learned to maintain eye contact with my audience and never to read from notes. Still, because I was nervous as hell, I needed a cheat sheet. So I handwrote my speech on four pages of hotel stationery, pages I still have, crumpled and dog-eared. On the evening of our arrival, Peter sat in rapt attention as I practiced my speech over and over, until the words, the pauses, the emotion flowed effortlessly. I was ready.

My hair, however, wasn't. After tossing my way through the night thanks to the five-hour time zone difference, I awakened to discover that my Parlux, a salon-quality dryer capable of defrizzing my mop, didn't bloody work. *Wrong converter.* That left me with the hotel's baby handheld, and a soggy mess on my head. In photos of me on the hearing day, you'll notice that my waves are neatly swept back. That was my only option with just a half hour to spare before go time. I wanted to appear in court dressed smartly, so I had steamed my outfit the evening before, a plaid suit and crisp white shirt, classic Lois Lane.

In the reception area, I met several survivors for the first time. Virginia Giuffre, whose 2015 case I had contributed to, warmly thanked me as we embraced. I recognized Courtney Wild from her many press interviews. We greeted. Many whom I'd never seen or known of trickled into the lobby, among the hotel's other guests. Without a word exchanged, I immediately knew who the survivors were. Their eyes spoke of buried traumas. Their expressions, artificially brightened, showed sadness in the backdrop. I know that wounding. I've worn that pretense. While we had been strangers before that Tuesday morning, these women were my kin. They, like me, had been to hell and back.

Those represented by my law firm, headed by David Boies, rode to the courthouse together. Renowned women's rights attorney Gloria Allred gathered with her group, as did other lawyers and their clients. We united on the steps of the courthouse named for Thurgood Marshall, the champion Supreme Court justice who dismantled Jim Crow. The courtroom was packed. Journalists, attorneys, survivors, family members sat knee to knee in the gallery. A row of chairs, designated for survivors to rotate through when it was our time to speak, faced the Honorable Judge Berman. William Sweeney, head of the FBI's New York office, and Geoffrey Berman, then New York's US attorney general (no relation to the judge), were there near the front. Maurene Comey, a prosecutor in the case against Epstein—and daughter of former FBI director James Comey—took her place alongside her team. At the defense table sat Jeffrey's attorneys, with an empty chair where the most notorious serial rapist in modern history would have sat, had he not been found dead eighteen days before. I studied the defense lawyers' faces, then and later, as the survivors spoke. No trace of compassion surfaced; in fact, as reporters and others gathered have noted, arrogance and insolence seemingly oozed from their pores. When Judge Berman entered, a hush fell and all rose.

"The victims have been included in the proceeding today, both because of their relevant experiences and because they should always be involved before, rather than after, the fact," he said. He emphasized how important it was, in the wake of Jeffrey's death—and even more so, because of it—for our accounts, our fury, our grievances to be aired following a 2008 secret plea deal that silenced so many. As he spoke, I glanced around, noticed survivors holding hands, welling up in anticipation of a day we never thought would come. There we sat trembling, a few of us publicly known, many simply identifying as Jane Doe to preserve their anonymity. Named or unnamed, we and our journeys overlapped, through a world, a land of sorrows, that nearly swallowed us whole.

One by one, tear by tear, each of us took to the podium. One Jane Doe described her time at Jeffrey's New Mexico ranch where, at age fifteen in 2004, her virginity was stolen by the then fifty-one-year-old pervert. "After he finished with me, he told me to describe in detail how good my first sexual experience felt," she said, and as the *New York Times* later reported. Jeffrey told her that he was helping her "to grow" by assaulting her. She spoke clearly, even if feebly. Some girls could hardly get through their memories before descending into sobs. A couple of them rambled, understandably so with agony long siloed away, while others whispered, mumbled, bellowed. One I suspected still had Stockholm syndrome, as she repeatedly referred to our rapist as "Jeff," with the ring of familiarity usually reserved for a friend. How each spoke, the force and timbre of her words, the vibration of the sound, revealed her place along the path to healing. I marveled at my sisters' courage. The emotion was both palpable and potent.

My heart pounded as my turn came to address the judge and court. I straightened my posture and stepped forward, Macpherson resolve coursing through me. "Your honor, my name is Sarah

Ransome," I said slowly, steeling myself, catching Peter's supportive eye. "I am a victim of Jeffrey Epstein and Ghislaine Maxwell's international sex-trafficking operation." *Pause. Breathe. You've got this.* "I would like to thank the court for the dignity and respect you are showing me, and all the victims today. I would also like to acknowledge and extend my gratitude to the prosecutors from the Southern District of New York for pursuing justice on behalf of the victims." *Gear shift.* "For a very long time, Jeffrey Epstein gamed the system at every level, and when he realized he couldn't do that any longer, he showed the world what a depraved and cowardly human being he is by taking his own life," I said, measuring each word. "But we, the victims, are still here, prepared to tell the truth, and we all know he did not act alone. We are survivors. The pursuit of justice should not abate. Please finish what you have started. Thank you." Judge Berman nodded and I took my seat, heart still racing, words midair. For twelve years I had waited to speak those sentences. In two minutes, a flurry of heartbeats strung together, my truth, my value, had been affirmed.

The testimonies, the unmuzzlings, filled an hour. Then William Sweeney and Geoffrey Berman led the survivors, and our attorneys, into a conference room. Sweeney choked back tears as he addressed the group, acknowledged how profoundly the government had failed us. I get goosebumps when I recall his heartfelt apology, spoken with emotion that cannot be faked. I glimpsed the regret on his and the others' faces. None of what was said would rewind time, blot out the violence we had endured. And yet their remorse, for me, served as a salve. They heard us. They believed us. They stood with us.

On my way from the courthouse, someone called my name. I turned to see a tall, beautiful young lady bounding toward me. "Oh my God, Sarah . . . I thought you were dead!" she said. I stared at her for a long moment, trying to place her. "Trina—is that you?" I asked. She nodded. I burst into tears. The ballet dancer, the one who had shared my bungalow, the one who'd vanished from my world once Jeffrey rotated her elsewhere, had grown from that eighteen-year-old frightened prey into a woman in her thirties. She remained caught in Jeffrey's web long after I escaped. The pain, those years, were etched on her brow. Our relationship had deteriorated on the island, with Jeffrey embracing her as his new golden girl of the moment. But here, on the outside, beyond the inferno, that history, that dynamic neither of us created, didn't matter. We had survived.

My emotions were all over the place as I packed to leave. Being back in New York laid to rest some traumas and resurrected others. *Where are Ghislaine, Sarah Kellen, Lesley Groff, Natalya Malyshev, the women who forced me to Jeffrey's suite door?* Their names went largely unspoken on that trip. During my plane ride back to Spain, and then once home, I held close the words I had uttered to the judge. *Please finish what you have started.* That plea, that prayer, has become my clarion call.

The strength of my voice, its reverberation, echoed and then trailed off. Back in Spain I sank into a depression that temporarily drained my life force. The adrenaline rush of pursuing Jeffrey had ended with his death. His conspirators' crimes, it seemed then, had been buried along with him. Sweeney and others spoke of an ongoing quest for justice, but would a reckoning ever come, and if so, when? Jeffrey and Ghislaine began procuring and grooming girls and young women all the way back in the nineties. The wheels of justice turn slowly, it has been said, and as they lag, rapists keep raping. It has to end.

That burning, that passion to take predators off our streets, eased my melancholy for a time. I poured my energy into press interviews, my way of creating a public archive of crimes committed by Ghislaine and others, of highlighting what I call Jeffrey & Company, an enterprise steered by women. I agreed to take part in the Netflix documentary *Jeffrey Epstein: Filthy Rich*. I spent long hours with the crew, shared details of my story I had not yet fully recounted, took them to an island cliff edge resembling the one where I had once attempted an ocean escape. I also participated in an interview with the BBC's *Panorama*. Both those interviews shined a spotlight on Jeffrey's enablers, a cross-examination they had mostly avoided.

One of my most memorable press experiences led to the cover of this book. In October 2019, a few months after Jeffrey's death, I did an interview with France 2, a public national television broadcast out of Paris. After my conversation with the crew, they requested that we drive to Jeffrey's duplex apartment on the exclusive Avenue Foch, near the Arc de Triomphe. Even after his death, the home was still attended by waitstaff, the thought of which filled me with disbelief. Who were these butlers, these housekeepers, these gardeners who continued servicing the property of a known international sex trafficker? I knocked on the door to find out. A gentleman answered, dressed as a butler. "I'm Sarah Ransome," I said just as boldly as I had in court. "I am a victim of Jeffrey Epstein and Ghislaine Maxwell's international sex-trafficking operation." Long pause. "Pardon, mademoiselle?" he said. I repeated my introduction, louder this time. The man sucked his teeth, muttered a slew of French insults, let out a boisterous laugh, and slammed the door in my face. I expected no different. I just hoped to bring attention, with the help of a film crew, to the many, possibly hundreds, complicit in Jeffrey & Company. It's unconscionable. And it should be called out.

Speaking out can empower. It can also drain. Every interview transported me to ground zero of my trauma. That's why I retreated for several months, breathed in more early morning air, pulled back from the public eye altogether. The world would soon join me in that grand time-out, as COVID-19 sent us all into lockdown. On March 15, 2020, Spain closed down. That whole period was as disorienting for me as it was for millions, the universe gone topsy-turvy overnight. Spain's version of the lockdown was not for the delicate. There were frequent patrols in our complex, to ensure that no one ventured outside. Police helicopters hovered about our nature reserve. Roads were blocked. Panic hung thick in the air. And of course there were the mask mandates, the runs on food and toiletries, the hours of isolation. Press conferences, shifting headlines, ICUs overflowing—every day was the same, yet no two were alike. It was all so maddening, yet strangely comforting for me, to feel part of a struggle touching everyone around the globe. If ever there was proof of our interconnectedness, it has come in these past two years. Community is central to our survival.

And then, that July, my earth shook again: Ghislaine had at last been tracked down and captured in New Hampshire, surprisingly to many who thought she may have absconded to France (she's a citizen there, and in Britain, and in America). On her bedside lay Bradley Edwards's book, *Relentless Pursuit: My Fight for the Victims of Jeffrey Epstein*. I thought the FBI had moved on from the Epstein-Maxwell case, had forgotten us survivors. But it hadn't. A second wave of euphoria washed over me, a deepening of the freedom that Jeffrey's death brought. Just as it had after the financier's arrest, the press pounced, with story after story on Ghislaine's involvement as Jeffrey's co-rapist. And just as I had then, I wished that the media had paid attention far sooner, during those years when Ghislaine was scouring Central Park for prey, claiming that she was on the lookout for Victoria's Secret models.

Ronan Farrow, the trailblazing journalist who broke the Harvey Weinstein story, among a plethora of others involving alleged sexual assault, has highlighted the media's role in reporting on such accounts. "Very often, women with allegations do not or cannot bring charges," he wrote in a 2016 *Hollywood Reporter* guest column, "My Father, Woody Allen, and the Danger of Questions Unasked." Ronan's sister Dylan Farrow has alleged that their father, Woody Allen, had "groomed" and sexually molested her when she was seven. The filmmaker has denied Dylan's claims and has never been legally convicted. "Very often, those who do come forward pay dearly, facing off against a justice system and a culture designed to take them to pieces," Ronan wrote. "A reporter's role isn't to carry water for those women. But it is our obligation to include the facts, and to take them seriously. Sometimes, we're the only ones who can play that role."

Whether or not the press does its part, I intend to do mine. Since Jeffrey's death and Ghislaine's arrest, my mission has become twofold. First, for full justice to be achieved against any criminal enterprise, the entire house of cards must topple. That's why the sisterhood of gymnasts in the Nassar case is calling for top-to-bottom accountability of everyone who was involved in the alleged cover-up, every person who turned a blind eye, every collaborator and abettor. "If we are to believe in change, we must first understand the problem and everything that contributed to it," said Olympic champion Aly Raisman at Nassar's hearing. "Now is not the time for false reassurances. We need an independent investigation of exactly what happened, what went wrong, and how it can be avoided for the future." I'm calling for something similar in the Epstein-Maxwell case: a thorough inquiry of those involved at every level of the pyramid, with the strongest examination for those in the top echelons—those who earned the most and meted out the greatest cruelties. Such accountability may or may not lead to conviction. But if conviction is warranted and implemented, that leads to my greatest intention in raising my voice: stopping predators before they can do more harm.

My second goal is to dramatically increase the amount of time victims have to report assailants' violations against them. I've had the privilege of working with renowned victims' rights advocate Robert Y. Lewis of the Marsh Law Firm. He likewise champions extending the statutes of limitations (SOLs) for reporting abuse. "For the last twenty or so years, sex abuse victims and their advocates have been lobbying state legislators to extend statutes of limitations for child sex abuse victims," he told me. "The argument is that on average, a person abused sexually as a child does not disclose the abuse to anyone until he or she is in his or her fifties, by which time the SOL in most states has long passed. Most states have SOL's requiring child sex abuse civil action to be brought by the time the survivor is twenty-one years old. We believe that in many states both criminal and civil SOLs for adult sex abuse survivors should be extended." In recent years, he says, several states have extended the SOLs; some have also "revived" those claims that were "dead" because of the passing of the SOL period. A revival statute, for example, would allow a forty-year-old abused as a child, who didn't file by the time he or she was twenty-one, to bring his or her claim within a window of a year or two.

"These are people who are so traumatized, they bury it," David Boies told the *New York Times*, in the article "Why These Five Accusers of Jeffrey Epstein Want More Than Money." David and his team have represented me and many other Epstein-Maxwell survivors. "To apply a quote 'normal' statute of limitations to that sort of conduct doesn't make any sense." Annie Farmer, one of the sisters who first took her claims against Epstein and Maxwell to the FBI, and who is now a psychologist, concurs. "It can take years or even decades for victims of sexual traumas to understand and process what has happened," she told the *New York Times*, in the same piece for which Boies commented. "In my case and in many cases where perpetrators hold positions of power, there is also significant and often warranted fear of retribution that can make the risks of a lawsuit feel too great." That fear, that deep foreboding, is another form of silencing—a wound of an emotional sort, a second fissure along the same fault line.

Britain, long part of the ensemble of voices making up the European Union, officially went solo in January 2020. After a transition period, Brexit was set to take effect in December of that year, at which point Peter and I, both British citizens, would have suddenly become undocumented migrants in Spain. With the influx of Brits returning home, housing was hard to come by. That scarcity sent prices soaring. I had no recent credit or rental history in the country, yet I was determined to get a place in my name, to begin reestablishing financial independence.

Our search began even before we left Spain. We didn't have the luxury of jumping on a plane for viewings. It was survival of the quickest on our keyboards. We would see a property online and call about it, only to hear it was already off the market. We finally found a house in the northern England countryside, in a lovely village dotted with birch and aspens. Within an hour of falling in love with the photos, I had paid a year's rent to secure it. We returned to Britain in November 2020, to a humble abode we'd never even seen. We arrived with one suitcase and waited in an empty house for our shipped belongings during a two-week quarantine. I'll forever be grateful to Liz, our kindhearted landlady, who left us the essentials we needed to survive. I was also thankful to converse in English again, after years on mute in Catalonia. And the most prized treasure, among other blessings, was our backyard garden. That next spring it brimmed with roses, foxgloves, and peonies, hummed with robins and sparrows. It has become my soul's refuge.

In my season of recovery, solitude beckoned. For the first time in my life, I didn't fear aloneness: I yearned for it. I needed to reflect, bathe in nature's stillness, as a way to begin healing. I adore Peter. I always will. This man has walked with me through hell's harrowing aftermath, resting his palm in the small of my back. Yet a few months after our return to England, we decided, together, to transition our romance into a dear friendship. He moved into his own place, and I moved into deeper quiet. The parting was as amicable as it was necessary, as requisite to my growth as was at last coming to terms with my father hunger. It was time.

I've spent so much of my life waiting: on a dad to show up and pull me close, on a prince to ride in and rescue me, on anyone, and any man in particular, to cast on me a warm ray of acceptance. My Father Wound is, in part, what created my desire for the Fairy Tale. Both still ache in unison at moments. For years, my dad and I have alternated between separation and combustion, aloofness and attachment. I long for his consistent gaze, our fingers interlaced, just as I did when I was a girl. He has offered it intermittently. Some of our distance, as I've laid bare in these pages, has been cemented by my own behavior; other parts of it remain inexplicable and painful. While I will always crave a cheek-to-cheek affection with the first man who ever held me, I leave space for that connection even as I move forward. I wait now on no earthly savior, no dashing knight or patriarch. I lean into the arms of Father God, whose presence is unfailing.

My mum and I have also entered a new season. When I returned to the UK, she was living in St. Margaret's Bay, a seaside Kent town several hours south of me. She didn't just want to move closer to her only daughter. She needed to. Winter is upon her, along with a continuing battle with alcoholism. So while I was relocating myself to England, I was also arranging her move to a house near mine during the COVID-19 lockdown. I am now my mum's caretaker, a role I resisted at earlier points in our relationship, but one I am learning to accept. Whatever my mother's imperfections have been, mine closely mirror them. However saddened I am by liquor's stranglehold on her, I am as certain now of her love as I was growing up. I am here, at her side, in recognition of that bond.

Our reunion has come with its stumbling blocks, made more jagged by addiction. On the day I told Mum I planned to pen this book, she stared at me for a long moment, wine glass in hand. "So I assume I'll be in it?" she asked rhetorically. I nodded yes, explained that sharing The Story, raw and bruising, required lifting the ancestral veil. "Well, I guess I'll have to come to terms with it then," she said. Such a reckoning extends for years, I can attest. For me, it has involved a look inward and around. My story, my mother's tale, and her mum and grandmother's Homeric sagas are all symbiotically connected, in ways both visible and disguised. I cannot know myself, in all of my historical fullness, until I peer into the lives of my foreparents, the rings in our oak that bear the grand plotline. When I can gaze at those rings with more grace than judgment, then I can begin accepting my own failings, and Mum's.

The path to healing winds through the land of hard truth,

through realities that initially blister. That temporary scorching, says spiritual teacher Iyanla Vanzant, is a prerequisite to liberation. "When you can look a thing dead in the eye, acknowledge that it exists, call it exactly what it is, and decide what role it will take in your life, then, my Beloved, you have taken the first step toward your freedom," she has said. Alcoholism is my "thing" to stare down. I did exactly that when I stepped into an AA meeting not long ago, recommitted to a sobriety I have since kept, while clinging to my serenity prayer. A dedication to sobriety is a decision to be present, fully awake to every peak and piercing. I want to be here for my life, all of it. I'm also taking part in psychodynamic therapy, an approach that brings relief to some trauma survivors. My results have been promising.

"You're at a major crossroads," my brother said when I told him of my twelve-step journey. James is living in Amsterdam now, working in corporate accounting, and offering me and Mum emotional support from afar. The turning point James spoke of is a long, slow arc I will navigate for years. My addiction is not about liquor, any more than a workaholic's compulsive pull toward the office is about work. It's about quieting the haunting voices that have echoed through my head since I was a girl: *You are damaged goods. You are to blame. You are worthless.* Replacing those beliefs is the spiritual work of my life.

Our world often urges us to look inward when seeking emotional equilibrium. While solitude is necessary for reflection, connection is the path to recovery. "For years mental health professionals taught people that they could be psychologically healthy without social support, that 'unless you love yourself, no one else will love you,'" writes Dr. Bruce Perry in *The Boy Who Was Raised as a Dog: And Other Stories from a Child Psychiatrist's Notebook*. "The truth is, you cannot love yourself unless you have been loved and are loved. The capacity to love cannot be built in isolation. . . . Relationships are the agents of change, and the most powerful therapy is human love."

My upbringing is a testament to that. I first saw my worth reflected in the eyes of my mum, felt it in the warmth of my nanny Miriam's embrace. I knew I mattered because I mattered to *them*. We humans stay alive for one another. I still struggle to build meaningful connections, an awkwardness I long eased with a glass of red. On this side of sobriety and sexual trauma, I am seeking out friendships. I am nurturing ties with women in my yoga classes. I am cherishing bonds with old mates around the world, even as I find new ones close by. Community, I am discovering, is a potent tonic.

Rape is a thief. Recovery involves reclamation of what has been stolen: your boundaries, your physical and emotional privates, your voice and conviction, your right to howl at monsters in your bed and at your side, your ability even to express fury at such blatant intrusions. The sense of safety many take for granted must be, for survivors, carefully reconstructed, breath by breath, stone by stone.

I reclaim, in these years, how I speak of myself and other trauma survivors. I am a victim of rape, yes, of a brutal sex-trafficking ring, but that is not all. I am also a fighter who has walked through hell and emerged from it, driven toward a purpose-filled calling to serve as a voice for others. We sisters who have, at times, been forced to trade our dignities for a bowl of hot soup are not "harlots" or "prostitutes," rubbish to be segregated, semantically or otherwise. We are survivors. We have done what we had to do, what we took no pleasure at all in doing, in order to remain here. For that we shouldn't be shamed and shunned. We should be regarded as warriors.

I take back, too, my perspective on my frailties. *Kintsugi*, the Japanese philosophy of embracing imperfection, of highlighting rather than hiding scars, flows from an ancient artistic tradition in which pieces of broken ceramic are melded together with gilded lacquer (*kintsugi* means "join with gold"). When a delicate vase crashes onto the floor, the shards are not discarded. They are restored, even celebrated, displayed on the mantel, mended and beautiful. That honoring says nothing of the hands that toppled the vase to its near ruin. It speaks only of its redemption, the grandeur in its new form. I am not "damaged goods." I am a perfectly imperfect human being with a right to stand in my humanity, to declare, amid a chorus of survivors, that we are worthy of being heard. Our pasts, our blemishes, should not bar us admittance from the human family. Our so-called defects, held together with precious metal, make us glorious additions.

Trauma has an opportunity cost. It robs not just one's present but also one's future self, the person who might have been, the monarch that may have flapped its brilliant orange wings. Courtney Wild was a fourteen-year-old cheerleader in braces, an *A* student, when a predator crossed her path. The assault violently cut off her forward motion and forever changed her direction. Like so many of us survivors, she later struggled with addiction as she tried to cope with overwhelming heartache. She can never retrieve those years, those possibilities. Maria Farmer, a painter, had her brush cruelly wrenched from her hand. Her career was stalled, her canvases sat empty. She can paint again, now and in the days to come, yet she cannot color over the earlier losses. Rape is a thief that keeps on stealing, a swindler of one's dignity and all that would have flowed from it. Such a burglar, a pillager of potential, should not roam freely in our midst.

Jeffrey and Ghislaine, and those who linked arms with them, stole the precious and the priceless. What remains is a gift, graced by heaven, that no human can ever destroy. The two most notorious accused predators of our time mutilated my spirit beyond recognition. Yet here I stand, bruised and undeterred, with a clarion call for justice. Things leveled rise up strong. Things shattered are not silenced.

ACKNOWLEDGMENTS

"If the only prayer you ever say in your entire life is thank you," philosopher Meister Eckhart once observed, "it will be enough." I offer that prayer to those who've walked alongside me—on my journey from silence to resonance, and on my path to publication.

Mum, I know we've had our ups and downs. With every year I grow older, I understand you more and have compassion for every hurt you've endured. It's never easy being a single mother, doing your very best to rear two children on your own. Amidst that struggle, you've succeeded in many ways. I recognize that now more than ever. You, like all of us, have had missteps, but you've compensated for all of them by standing in my corner and fighting for me when others would not. I've also made my own mistakes, plentiful and painful. I hope we can work through our demons and walk, however slowly, toward healing. I love you, Mum.

Peter, you've been my lifeline, confidant, and best friend. I've tested you to the limits, pushing you to walk away from me like the rest before I could really trust you. You stood your ground and never left my side. You have my friendship, my companion-ship, and my respect. You are a good soul.

James, thank you for always having your little sister's back—for supporting me when you knew it mattered, and when others turned away. Integrity, courage, and honesty make us who we are. You have demonstrated such character. I love you, Jamo.

Lisa Bryant of Radical Media, and director of *Filthy Rich* on Netflix: Thank you for your determination in seeking out the truth, and for your dedication to the survivors. You have become a cherished friend.

To my **close-knit friends** who have supported me through the years . . . you know who you are. Your friendship and loyalty are invaluable to me. You've given me the strength to move forward, with a renewed sense of purpose.

Steve Ross, you are so much more than an outstanding literary agent, the best in the business. You are also a gifted and kind soul. This book simply would not have been possible without your ex-traordinary support and enthusiasm. Thank you for being the first to believe in my story, and for championing its publication at every turn. Your great compassion as a person is equaled only by your immense experience as a publishing professional. Both have served as my lampposts. I hope we'll work together for many years to come.

To the **HarperCollins book team**, headed by the inimitable **Judith Curr**: Thank you for standing so powerfully at my side in our shared mission, removing the shame and stigma so many survivors experience when they valiantly step forward. Judith, you immediately recognized the need for this narrative to exist, and for that, I will forever be grateful. To my editor, **Gideon Weil**, you have invested your considerable talent in ensuring my story resonates. Thank you for your warmth and patience, as well as for your professional skill as we've navigated our way to publication. I am personally appreciative of you, your team, and the many long hours you've devoted to me and to this memoir. I am also quite grateful to **Paul Olsewski**, senior director of publicity, as well as to the dozens of others—the production team, the sales and marketing forces, the art directors—who have poured themselves into this project. Your efforts, behind the scenes and out front, are valued.

Bradley Edwards, thank you from the bottom of my heart for your decades-long dedication and personal sacrifices on behalf of dozens of survivors in our fight for justice. You've never given up on us, and without your deep commitment, our voices would not have been heard. I really value our friendship and the time you've always made for me throughout the years.

David Boies, Sigrid McCawley, and the team at Boies Schiller Flexner: I sincerely appreciate your phenomenal efforts and legal prowess in representing me and scores of other survivors. Your advice, partnership, and advocacy have been critical.

James R. Marsh and Robert Y. Lewis of Marsh Law Firm: Thank you for stepping forward and helping me at a key juncture in my journey. You have shown me dignity and respect, and I am exceedingly grateful. Going forward, I hope we can continue working together in our fight to change laws that protect perpetrators.

Paul G. Cassell, thank you for taking my first call and hearing my voice when I came forward in 2016. Your years of expertise and ongoing commitment to justice are very much recognized, admired, and respected.

To the **brave survivors** whose stories I've included in these pages, and to the millions of trauma survivors all over the world: I see you. I hear you. I thank you for your incredible courage and candor. And I stand with you.